Praise for Work and

"God commands us to work. And Scott LaPierre shows how the Bible discloses the sinfulness of laziness and 'idleness,' and he unpacks the contrary biblical virtue of 'diligence.' But he also shows how our relationship to work can become sinful. Workaholism turns work into an addiction that can lead to burnout and idolatry. The biblical principle of the Sabbath counters those tendencies with physical rest, the cessation of busyness necessary for spiritual devotion, and the life of faith, in which we realize that our salvation comes not by our work, but by resting in Christ. *Work and Rest God's Way* is a welcome contribution as Christians rediscover the doctrine of vocation in all of its practicality and spiritual richness."

Dr. Gene Edward Veith—Provost at Patrick Henry College, director of the Cranach Institute at Concordia Theological Seminary, and author of *God at Work*

"*In Work and Rest God's Way,* Scott LaPierre wonderfully reconciles the very real tension between work and rest by resisting the celebrated extremes of workaholism and play by relying on the principles and patterns laid out in God's Word. In an age when so many are sacrificing so much to gain so very little—manifested through materialism on the one hand and hedonism on the other— this book will help you, especially if you're a young man, navigate this life-altering strait."

Kirk Smith—Church planter, pastor, and Executive Director for the Illinois Christian Home Educators (ICHE)

"Scott LaPierre has produced a much-needed resource to help our churches and families recognize the blessing and purpose of work. He addresses sloth, the penalty for it and overwork and the need to rest, ultimately finding our rest in Christ."

Gary Powers—Preaching elder and founder and CEO of Ortho Molecular Products

WORK AND REST GOD'S WAY

WORK AND REST GOD'S WAY

*A Biblical Recipe for Finding Joy and Purpose
in All You Do*

Scott LaPierre

www.scottlapierre.org | scott@scottlapierre.org

ISBN: 0-9995551-3-8
ISBN 13: 978-0-9995551-3-2
Library of Congress Control Number: 2019913271
Charis Publishing

Unless otherwise indicated, all Scripture quotations are taken from the New King James Version®, copyright © 1982 by Thomas Nelson. Used by permission. All rights reserved.

Abbreviations used for other versions:

- ESV—The ESV® Bible (The Holy Bible, English Standard Version®) copyright © 2001 by Crossway, a publishing ministry of Good News Publishers. ESV® Text Edition: 2011. The ESV® text has been reproduced in cooperation with and by permission of Good News Publishers. Unauthorized reproduction of this publication is prohibited. All rights reserved.
- NASB—Scripture taken from the NEW AMERICAN STANDARD BIBLE®, copyright © 1960, 1962, 1963, 1968, 1971, 1972, 1973, 1975, 1977, 1995 by The Lockman Foundation. Used by permission.
- NIV—THE HOLY BIBLE, NEW INTERNATIONAL VERSION®, NIV®, copyright © 1973, 1978, 1984, 2011 by Biblica, Inc.®. Used by permission. All rights reserved worldwide.

Scripture quotations with brackets, parentheses, or italics are the emphasis of the author.

Dedication

Work and Rest God's Way is dedicated to the hardest working people I know—bi-vocational pastors.

Acknowledgments

First, I want to thank Kandie Schmitz, D.G. Angelynn, Kirk VanGelder, Eamonn Ryan, Anna Templin, and my children for serving as beta readers. Your contributions were invaluable.

Second, I want to thank my Lord and Savior, Jesus Christ. You save us apart from our works, and then You allow us to serve You. As if that isn't enough, You even provide the works for us to do:

> For by grace you have been saved through faith. And this is not your own doing; it is the gift of God, *not a result of works*, so that no one may boast. For we are his workmanship, created in Christ Jesus *for good works, which God prepared beforehand, that we should walk in them* (Ephesians 2:8–10).

Foreword

"No one likes doing more than they absolutely must."

When my fourteen-year-old son shared this sentiment with me after doing his chores poorly, my mind flashed back to when I was his age. As I engaged him, I couldn't help but reminisce on what had changed my perspective. I began working full-time outside the home the week I turned sixteen. As the only son of a single-parent mother, I felt a great responsibility to help provide for the financial needs of her and my five sisters. Life dictated that I become a man early.

My first impression upon working forty-to-fifty hours per week was that I was going to die! I was so tired all the time. My muscles weren't used to the physical strain, and my brain wasn't used to waking up so early. One of the upsides of being homeschooled was being able to set my own schedule and work at my own pace. One of the downsides was that I hadn't learned to be regimented. Being thrown into the deep end of the pool (metaphorically speaking) and told to swim was good for me, and my mother knew it. Continuing my education in the workplace was a way for me to add to the wonderful education I received at home.

What I hadn't picked up in my schoolwork or church attendance was a scriptural understanding of work. At that young age, I hadn't yet discovered that there was a biblical theology for, well, everything!

As my mind returned to my son who was sitting in front of me trying to give a defense for why he had done a half-hearted job, I realized that it was a combination of two forces that caused me to tell him, "I actually like doing more than I must."

The first force for good in my life was simply the work itself. God created us to work, so when we exert ourselves and press past the initial resistance, we usually find pleasure in it. It is part of our worship, fulfilling a major purpose for our existence. Isaac

Newton's principle of physics, "Objects in motion tend to stay in motion, and objects at rest tend to stay at rest" is true of humans as well. Getting moving is the most difficult aspect. As the old sneaker ad used to say, "Just do it!" Doing meaningful work and seeing progress being made spurs us on to do more.

As is the case with most of life, we can be led by either our emotions or our will. Being led by our will means we must engage our minds with what is true. The body says it's tired, so the mind must tell the body that it should keep working. For that to happen, there must be a plumb line for what a "should" even looks like. In other words, we need a standard that tells us what is right and wrong regarding work and rest. What is healthy, and what is obsessive? What is servanthood, and what is self-seeking? Are we ultimately working for God or for ourselves? What is the purpose and meaning of work?

To be driven by the correct motivations, we must develop a biblical theology of work. The God who created work blessed it, gave it to us as a gift, and has also provided a blueprint in the Bible for how we should view and engage in work. Our goal, then, is to seek it out, and apply it effectively in our lives.

The great news is that the heavy lifting for such a study has been largely done for us! Scott LaPierre, in the pages of *Work and Rest God's Way*, lays out the biblical guidelines for how we should think about labor, productivity, and rest. Having done much of the research on our behalf, we get the luxury of quickly and easily absorbing the concepts in a concise format.

As a father of ten, I am looking forward to incorporating these important truths into the training of my own children. Parenting involves both formal teaching and example. It's a blessing to have a resource that can help them think correctly about work. Rather than seeing it as a curse and, therefore, something to be avoided (as much of even the Christian world does), they can begin to see it as a blessing if kept within its proper confines and restraints.

This is a great discipleship tool for families and churches that will help us think "Christianly" about our relationship to our vocational callings. It is my prayer that this book will lead a generation into not only thinking correctly about this important issue but also living in such a way that a watching world "may see your good works and glorify your Father in heaven" (Matthew 5:16).

Israel Wayne—Author, conference speaker, and director of Family Renewal, LLC

Contents

Introduction

My dad is one of the hardest working people I know. We grew up on a few acres in the mountains of northern California, and he always found plenty for us to do. School was more restful for me than being home. While most kids looked forward to weekends and summers, I didn't. I knew it meant one thing: work.

I played sports throughout the year because it got me out of working, but there were no sports during the summer. Since I knew I'd be working if I was home, I got a job as quickly as possible because at least then I'd get paid. For one summer, I worked two jobs: bagging groceries at Safeway during the day, followed by waiting tables at a restaurant in the evening. Once, on the way to my second job, I was so exhausted I fell asleep behind the wheel and crashed into the truck in front of me. I remember waking up on a stretcher in the middle of the road with paramedics leaning over me. By God's grace, I didn't kill anyone, but I totaled my parents' new Isuzu Rodeo.

Working Myself to Death

After college, I served as an Army Officer, an elementary school teacher, and then I went into ministry. When I became the senior pastor of Woodland Christian Church in 2010, I had no idea how much work was involved in shepherding a church. By 2013, the church had grown, and my days (and nights) were packed with activities such as studying, teaching, counseling, making phone calls, responding to emails, administrative responsibilities, visitations, and benevolence issues. I rarely had a day off. Sunday would conclude, and then on Monday morning, I'd begin another exhausting week of trying to get everything completed before the following Sunday rolled around.

The stress took a toll on me. I'd wake up in the middle of the night, unable to fall back asleep because my mind was occupied with the work that needed to be done. I lost thirty pounds and started having anxiety attacks. There was constant pain and tightness in my chest. I'd go to bed and wonder if I'd wake up again in the morning. No one has ever wanted me to be a pastor more than my wife, Katie, but my anxiety worried her. She started encouraging me to go back to teaching. She was afraid she was going to lose her husband, and our kids were going to lose their father.

Trusting God's Word

Why do I mention all the above? Is it supposed to make you think the following chapters are going to push you to work as hard as you can, and as often as you can? No. Much of this book is committed to the importance of physical and spiritual rest.

Instead, I hope to have some credibility with you while discussing work and rest. I have experienced firsthand the blessings of obedience and the consequences of disobedience in these areas. Let me acknowledge that I'm also more than familiar with laziness. There are many times I don't feel like working, helping my wife, getting out of bed, or serving people in the church. I need the same encouragement from the Bible as much as everyone else.

This brings me to my last point. I'm asking you to trust God's Word through my writing. *Work and Rest God's Way* is not a collection of my personal thoughts and opinions. Instead, it is filled with Scripture—truth I've labored over for my flock and for myself, and truth that has led me to conclude that God knows what is best for us. I look forward to sharing this truth with you in the following chapters.

Chapter One

Understanding Morality

During college, I took a world religions class. A Buddhist monk was brought in as a guest speaker. He had no vehicle, computer, or refrigerator because he thought these were sinful (immoral). He thought it was good (moral) to allow himself only what was necessary for survival, such as food, water, and shelter.

This is not what Jesus meant when He said, "If anyone desires to come after Me, let him deny himself, and take up his cross daily, and follow Me" (Luke 9:23). Jesus referred to denying ourselves immoral pleasures, but the monk abstained from the amoral (nonsinful, spiritually neutral). Colossians 2:20–23 records:

> Therefore, if you died with Christ from the basic
> principles of the world, why, as though living in the
> world, do you subject yourselves to regulations—"Do
> not touch, do not taste, do not handle," which all
> concern things which perish with the using—
> according to the commandments and doctrines of
> men? These things indeed have an appearance of
> wisdom in self-imposed religion, false humility, and
> neglect of the body, but are of no value against the
> indulgence of the flesh.

When people rigorously neglect the amoral and follow legalistic, man-made commands, Paul acknowledged there's "an appearance of wisdom," but there's "no value against [indulging] the flesh," which is to say there's no spiritual benefit. How heartbreaking is it for people to spend years rigorously neglecting themselves in amoral ways that have no moral advantage?

The Bible teaches drunkenness and homosexuality are immoral (1 Corinthians 6:9–10). How tragic is it for people to spend years getting drunk or participating in homosexual relationships because they're convinced these immoral actions are amoral?

We must understand morality because if we don't, we might fail to see the goodness (morality) of certain behaviors and the sinfulness (immorality) of other behaviors. The above examples demonstrate the two errors we typically make with morality.

Error 1: Thinking Something Is Immoral When It Is Amoral

What we do with food, guns, and money is moral because each can be used in moral and immoral ways. Our relationships with them are moral because they can become idols, addictions, and obsessions. Although, as lifeless and inanimate objects, they have no morality of their own. People are not spiritually better or worse if they do or don't eat certain foods, have or don't have guns, or are rich or poor.

Certain foods are healthier and unhealthier than others, but spiritually they're not better or worse than others. Paul said, "Food does not commend us to God; for neither if we eat are we the better, nor if we do not eat are we the worse" (1 Corinthians 8:8).[1] Food is amoral, but our relationship to it is moral. We can commit the sin of gluttony or, on the other side of the spectrum, the sins of

---

[1] See also Matthew 15:11, Mark 7:18, Acts 10:15, Romans 14:17, and Colossians 2:16–23.

anorexia and bulimia. God doesn't care what we eat, but He cares how much we eat.

Money is amoral, despite the famous quote: "Money is the root of all evil." First Timothy 6:10 says, "For the love of money is a root of all kinds of evil, for which some have strayed from the faith in their greediness, and pierced themselves through with many sorrows." Notice that the word "money" is substituted for "love of money," and "the root of all evil" is substituted for "a root of all kinds of evil." Although the differences seem small, they make two untrue statements.

First, the love of money versus money itself is evil. We are not better or worse if we're rich or poor. We get into trouble when money controls us, regardless of how much wealth we have. Some of the most generous people can be the wealthiest, while some of the stingiest can be the poorest.

Second, the quote makes money responsible for all evil in the world, but there's plenty of sin that has nothing to do with money. Jesus said evil comes from our hearts versus money: "For out of the heart proceed evil thoughts, murders, adulteries, fornications, thefts, false witness, blasphemies" (Matthew 15:19). Sin is not birthed from money but from giving in to temptation: "Each one is tempted when he is drawn away by his own desires and enticed. Then, when desire has conceived, it gives birth to sin; and sin, when it is full-grown, brings forth death" (James 1:14–15).

Error 2: Thinking Something Is Amoral When It Is Moral or Immoral

Many verses discuss the morality of our words. For example:

- Matthew 12:37—Jesus said, "For by your words you will be justified, and by your words you will be condemned."
- 1 Peter 3:10—He who would love life and see good days, let him refrain his tongue from evil, and his lips from speaking deceit.

Most people know their speech is moral, but they might not know that the amount they speak and the amount they listen is also moral. James 1:19 says, "So then, my beloved brethren, let every man be swift to hear, slow to speak, slow to wrath." The verse contains three commands, which means we're dealing with morality. It is moral to be quick to hear, slow to speak, and slow to anger. It is immoral to be slow to hear, quick to speak, and quick to anger. Anger and listening might be mentioned together because they're closely related. As a pastor, when I'm counseling, sometimes it's obvious early on who's more at fault because they're slow to hear and quick to get angry.

Ecclesiastes teaches that one way to identify fools is they talk too much: "A fool's voice is known by his many words...a fool also multiplies words" (Ecclesiastes 5:3 and 10:14). David took so seriously how much he said that he prayed God would protect his mouth for him: "Set a guard, O LORD, over my mouth; keep watch over the door of my lips" (Psalm 141:3).

Proverbs is filled with contrasts between wise and foolish people. One of the contrasts is wise people listen, but foolish people babble on: "The wise in heart will receive commands, but a prating fool will fall" (Proverbs 10:8).[2] Another contrast is a theme of this book: wise people work hard, but foolish people are lazy.

The Morality of Work

Bob Black, an American anarchist and author, wrote in his essay, *The Abolition of Work*:

> No one should ever work. Work is the source of nearly all the misery in the world. Almost any evil you'd care to name comes from working or from living in a world

---

[2] See also Proverbs 10:19, 13:3, and 17:27–28.

designed for work. In order to stop suffering, we have to stop working.[i]

Not only does Black think work is immoral, he thinks it's the cause of all suffering.

How do we determine whether this author is correct in his assessment? How do we know if work is moral, immoral, or amoral? We look to the Bible because it is the authority on morality. The question is not, "What does Bob, or me, or you, or anyone else think is moral, immoral, or amoral?" The question is, "What does the Bible teach?" Morality (or goodness) is defined by God. Psalm 100:5 says, "For the Lord is good."[3] Good is what God does, and what God does is good.

Work Is Good Because God Works

Just as listening and speaking are moral, so is work. The Bible opens with God working: "In the beginning God created the heavens and the earth" (Genesis 1:1). Then Genesis 2:2–3 records:

> And on the seventh day God ended *His work* which He had done, and He rested on the seventh day from all *His work* which He had done. Then God blessed the seventh day and sanctified it, because in it He rested from all *His work* which God had created and made.

The words "His work" occur three times in two verses. God is the first worker, revealing work is good and moral!

God's Work Brings Him Glory

Psalm 19:1 says, "The heavens declare the glory of God; and the firmament shows *the work of His hands*." God's work is creative, purposeful, thorough, and it benefits us: "For You, Lord, have made me glad through *Your work*; I will triumph in *the works of Your hands*"

---

[3] See also 1 Chronicles 16:34, Psalm 25:8, 34:8, 86:5, 135:3, and 145:7.

(Psalm 92:4). Jesus said, "My Father *has been working* until now, and I *have been working*" (John 5:17).

Isaiah 6 showcases the wonderful vision of God sitting on His throne, high and lifted up, with the train of His robe filling the temple. Angels fly around Him, and Isaiah 6:3 says, "One cried to another and said: 'Holy, holy, holy is the Lord of hosts; the whole earth is *full of His glory!*'" Creation is the display case for God's work.

Romans 1:20 says, "For since the creation of the world His invisible attributes are clearly seen, being understood by the things that are made, even His eternal power and Godhead, so that they are without excuse." The greatness of creation reveals the greatness of the Creator. God reveals Himself to the world by His creation because work reveals something about the worker. Work speaks of character, motivation, and skills. God's work is of the highest quality because it is an expression of who He is.

Our Work Should Bring God Glory

We should work because God works. Genesis 1:27 says, "So God created man in His own image; in the image of God He created him; male and female He created them." We are made in the image of God with some of His attributes. We work because we are His image-bearers! Ephesians 5:1 commands us to "be imitators of God." To work is to be like God because it reflects what He does.

In Isaiah 43:7, God said, "Everyone...I have created *for My glory*," which is why in 1 Corinthians 10:31 Paul said, "Whether you eat or drink, or whatever you do, do all *to the glory of God*." Giving glory to God means representing Him well; therefore, the work we do should give others an exalted view of God. Since God's work is of the highest quality, our work should be of the highest quality. We strive for excellence because our work says something about the God we represent. Jesus said, "Let your light so shine before men, that they may *see your good works and glorify your Father in heaven*" (Matthew 5:16). Why do we work as though our work brings God glory? Because it does! People look on, see our work, and when it is done well, it gives glory to God.

Colossians 3:23 says, "And whatever you do, do it heartily, *as to the Lord* and not to men, knowing that from the Lord you will receive the reward of the inheritance; for *you serve the Lord Christ.*" Why do we work as though we're working for Christ? Because we are! Ephesians 6:7 says that we work "with goodwill doing service, *as to the Lord*, and not to men." Even when performing jobs that might seem menial or insignificant, we should do our best because we're doing them for the Lord. Our work ethic is one of our greatest testimonies. We must view our occupations as ministries, and our workplaces as mission fields, whether we're in an office building, school, or our home. Our work is done God's way when it's done for His glory!

Work Is a Blessing Versus a Punishment

We might have expected Jesus to spend all His time in the temple worshiping, praying, discussing Scripture, and doing other things that seem spiritual. Instead, He worked as a carpenter with His earthly father, Joseph, before beginning His public ministry (Mark 6:3). The Son of God Himself worked, and so did other great men in Scripture. Paul was as a tentmaker (Acts 18:1–3). Luke was a physician (Colossians 4:14).

God called people to serve Him when they were working. Moses was caring for sheep (Exodus 3:1). Joshua was Moses' servant before he became his successor (Exodus 33:11). Gideon was threshing wheat (Judges 6:11). David was caring for his father's sheep (1 Samuel 16:11). Jesus called four men to serve as His disciples while they were fishing (Luke 5:1–11).

For others, their professions aren't listed, but they worked so hard for God's kingdom that Paul named them in his letters! For example, Tabitha "was full of good works and charitable deeds"

(Acts 9:36). Euodia, Syntyche, and Clement were praised because they "labored with [Paul]" (Philippians 4:2–3). Epaphroditus worked so hard he nearly died (Philippians 2:30). Tryphena, Tryphosa, and Persis were commended for their hard work for the Lord (Romans 16:12).

God created us to work. Genesis 2:15 says, "Then the LORD God took the man and put him in the garden of Eden to tend and keep it." God gave Adam the job of dressing and guarding the garden. What does this original work mandate mean? To "tend" means to foster growth and to improve. To "keep" means to preserve from failure or decline.

Genesis 1:31 says, "Then God saw everything that He had made, and indeed it was very good. So, the evening and the morning were the sixth day." God gave Adam work to do on the sixth day, which means it is also "very good." The timing is important: sin hadn't been introduced. Since this is prior to The Fall, it demonstrates work is not part of the curse. Instead, it is part of God's perfect creation.

"Tending and keeping" Eden was designed to be a pleasant experience for Adam. He was meant to find his work fulfilling, purposeful, and rewarding. God created man to enjoy work so that He could enjoy watching him, just as parents enjoy watching their children do something positive and productive.

Just as God observed His work and was satisfied with it, we can have the same experience from our work. Few things are more fulfilling than accomplishing a lengthy task or finishing a difficult job. Animals are motivated by instinct and physical need, but we have higher motivations than simply surviving. We crave meaning, significance, and purpose. We want reasons to get up in the morning. Work gives us these reasons and helps fulfill our desires.

We should embrace the work God has given us, and express gratitude to Him that work allows us to:

- Provide for ourselves and our families

- Experience satisfaction and fulfillment
- Develop character and endurance
- Make discoveries about God's creation
- Advance the kingdom through our talents

Work is an important part of life. Remembering the above blessings allows us to view work as a gift. Then we can work joyfully and without complaint, finding pleasure and giving thanks.

Second only to Jesus, Solomon was the wisest man to ever live. In Ecclesiastes 2:24, he said, "Nothing is better for a man than that he should eat and drink, and that his soul should enjoy good in his labor. This also, I saw, was from the hand of God." Solomon makes the same point four other times, in Ecclesiastes 3:12, 5:18, 8:15, and 9:7. God does not use highlighting, italics, underlining, or bold for emphasis, but He does repeat Himself when He wants to make sure we don't miss something. He wants us to know that along with eating and drinking (or the simple things in life), "nothing is better" for us than that "[our] soul enjoy" our work.

Consequences of The Fall

Unfortunately, over the centuries, work has developed a negative reputation. We often view it as something that we are forced to perform that is difficult or unpleasant. How did something positive become viewed negatively? If we take our minds back to The Fall, God pronounced several judgments. To man He said:

> Cursed is the ground for your sake; in toil you shall eat of it all the days of your life. Both thorns and thistles it shall bring forth for you, and you shall eat the herb of the field. In the sweat of your face you shall eat bread till you return to the ground, for out of it you were taken; for dust you are, and to dust you shall return (Genesis 3:17–19).

Work figures centrally in the judgments. God still expects man to work after The Fall, but the pleasant experience has been replaced with drudgery and discomfort. The word "toil" implies challenge, difficulty, struggle, and exhaustion. Work itself is still good, but the process and the result are not always positive. Hard work is not always rewarded in the way we expect or desire. We sow seed, but the plants grow among thorns and weeds.

Eden was created by God as an earthly paradise. It was a safe enclosure with purity and innocence. As a result of The Fall, instead of working in the garden, we're forced to work "of the field." Unlike the garden, the field represents an unbounded, unprotected area with less inhibition and more worldliness. We face greater hostility in our work environments, simply because we're Christians. Think of the opposition Joseph faced working in Egypt (Genesis 39), the Hebrews faced in Egypt (Exodus 1:8–22), and the Jews faced when they returned to the land (Nehemiah 4).

God's original design for work was ruined by sin, but God will restore it to its pre-Fall condition without the burdens The Fall introduced. Regarding the coming kingdom:

> They shall build houses and inhabit them; they shall plant vineyards and eat their fruit. They shall not build and another inhabit; they shall not plant and another eat; for as the days of a tree, so shall be the days of My people, and My elect shall *long enjoy the work of their hands. They shall not labor in vain"* (Isaiah 65:21–23).

Work that was previously painstaking will again be pleasant. After the consequences of The Fall are removed, we continue working. Revelation 22:3 says, "There shall be no more curse, but the throne of God and of the Lamb shall be in it, *and His servants shall serve Him."* Even in heaven, we continue serving God, but no longer encumbered by the curse. We see that whether before the curse, during the curse, or after the curse, God expects us to work.

12

The Immorality of Laziness

One of the other consequences of The Fall is the sinful nature we received. The curse made work unpleasant, so we're tempted toward laziness. Since God commands us to work, failure to do so is sinful.

When we think of the "worst" sins, lying, adultery, and murder come to mind, but laziness might not. Some people don't even recognize laziness is a sin. This is unfortunate because:

- As moral as work is, laziness is equally immoral
- As beneficial as work is, laziness is equally detrimental
- As positively as Scripture presents work, laziness is presented equally negatively

Ronald Sailler and David Wyrtzen wrote, "Laziness could run a competitive race for the most underrated sin. Quietly it anesthetizes its victim into a lifeless stupor that ends in hunger, bondage, and death."[ii] Though laziness is a sin that has no place in the character of a Christian, like pride, dishonesty, unforgiveness, and anxiety, it is a sin that all of us can identify with to some extent. Laziness might be a more difficult struggle for some than for others, but nobody can say they escape its temptation completely.

If we appreciate the morality of work, we'll be better prepared to resist the temptation to be lazy. The other beneficial component is an accurate view of the immorality of laziness. The following chapter provides the needed information to avoid laziness and embrace working God's way!

A Tragic Example of Laziness

Perhaps no other individual in all of Scripture can sober us to the seriousness of laziness than the third servant in the parable of the talents. Matthew 25:14–23 records:

> For the kingdom of heaven is like a man traveling to a far country, who called his own servants and delivered his goods to them. And to one he gave five talents, to another two, and to another one, to each according to his own ability; and immediately he went on a journey. Then he who had received the five talents went and traded with them, and made another five talents. And likewise he who had received two gained two more also. But he who had received one went and dug in the ground, and hid his lord's money. After a long time the lord of those servants came and settled accounts with them.
> So he who had received five talents came and brought five other talents, saying, "Lord, you delivered to me five talents; look, I have gained five more talents besides them." His lord said to him, "Well done, good and faithful servant; you were faithful over a few things, I will make you ruler over many things. Enter into the joy of your lord." He also who had received two talents came and said, "Lord, you delivered to me

two talents; look, I have gained two more talents besides them." His lord said to him, "Well done, good and faithful servant; you have been faithful over a few things, I will make you ruler over many things. Enter into the joy of your lord."

The "man" is Jesus, and the trip "to a far country" is His return to heaven. The master expects the men to carry on the work He started; therefore, He gave them talents.

Since God distributes the talents, we might expect Him to give each person the same amount. Instead, one received five, another two, and the third only one. The application is God does not have the same expectations for everyone. Some people will produce less than others, but if they are faithful, they will receive the same reward as those who produced more. The parable demonstrates this in that the man who returned two talents heard the same words as the first servant: "Well done, good and faithful servant; you were faithful over a few things, I will make you ruler over many things. Enter into the joy of your lord" (Matthew 25:21 and 23). Although producing less than half as much as the first servant he received the same commendation, because he was equally faithful—he also doubled what he was given.

The sad situation with the third servant follows in Matthew 25:24–28:

> Then he who had received the one talent came and said, "Lord, I knew you to be a hard man, reaping where you have not sown, and gathering where you have not scattered seed. And I was afraid, and went and hid your talent in the ground. Look, there you have what is yours."
> But his lord answered and said to him, "You wicked and lazy servant, you knew that I reap where I have not sown, and gather where I have not scattered seed. So you ought to have deposited my money with the bankers, and at my coming I would have received

back my own with interest. So take the talent from him, and give it to him who has ten talents."

The third servant made two strong accusations, and then the excuse that he was afraid. First, he said the master was cruel and expected more from his servants than he should: "I knew you to be a hard man." Second, he said the master took what didn't belong to him: "reaping where he hadn't sown, and gathering where he hadn't scattered." In the servant's estimation, the master had no business claiming what he didn't produce.

Knowing God Is Severe Makes Us More Accountable

There is no getting around that God is severe, and we don't have to try to get around it anyway, because He wants us to know this about Him. Romans 11:22 says, "*Consider* the goodness and *severity of God*: on those who fell, severity; but toward you, goodness, if you continue in His goodness. Otherwise you also will be cut off." We're told to "Consider," "Note" (ESV), or "Behold" (NASB) God's severity, and few places in Scripture demonstrate it as graphically as the punishment reserved for the lazy servant: "Cast [him] into the outer darkness. There will be weeping and gnashing of teeth" (Matthew 25:30).

While the master's joy was evident with the previous two servants, including inviting them to experience His joy with Him, with the third servant, there's an absence of joy. It's quite the contrast: joy to indignation. Why? Part of the reason is contained in the words, "you knew." The servant knew the master was severe but disobeyed Him anyway. The master put a hole in the man's logic. If the servant knew the master was "a hard man," that was more reason for him to be faithful. The servant's words backfired and sealed his fate.

If lazy people could excuse themselves, they might sound like the third servant: "I didn't serve you because I know you're a God who judges people." This argument fails, because if they know God judges people, they have even more reason to be faithful. Sometimes people say, "What kind of God would…" and then they list criticisms like, "Keep people out of heaven…send people to hell…punish them." The answer is, "The kind of God you should fear!" The third servant had no fear of the master. If he did, he would've at least deposited his talent with the bankers so it could gain interest.

The master repeated back some of what the servant said. He left out the words that weren't true, such as "a hard man." Up to this point, the master's behavior suggested the opposite. He gave talents to his servants, which made him look generous. The talents were appropriate to their ability levels, which made him look fair. Then He rewarded them, which made him look gracious.

He repeated the words that were true, such as, "I reap where I have not sown, and gather where I have not scattered seed." This summarizes the parable. The master expects us to work and provide Him with fruit from seed He didn't plant. He gives us talents, so he can have a return on his investment.

Does this make God unfair? It shouldn't because we have the same expectation. Think of an investment manager. You give him money, and in the future, you expect him to return more money than you gave him. How angry would you be if you asked for your money and the investment manager said, "You're such a difficult investor I didn't invest your money for you. Here! Take back what you gave me!" We'd be frustrated, and we might even say, "You could have at least invested it in a savings account so that I'd receive some interest!" God feels the same way with us.

The Master Might Not Expect Much, but He Expects Something

There are two sides to the master's expectations: one encouraging and the other sobering. Since the first two servants doubled their investment, it can look like the master has high expectations. We might be inclined to think He'll only be pleased if we also produce a considerable amount and double our investment too. But then the third servant is judged and the master reveals he would've been satisfied with only interest! You don't have to be a banker to know that interest isn't very much. This is encouraging because it shows a considerably lower bar can satisfy the master.

The third servant received only one talent. If anyone looks as though he could get by without working, it's this servant because he was given so little. But God still expected something from him. This is sobering. Nobody can ever say, "Well, God didn't give me much in the way of gifts or talents, so why even bother? If I had five talents, or even two, I'd work for the Lord, but since I only have one, I can be lazy." The master's pronouncement against the third servant shows this excuse won't work.

The master wasn't upset that the servant only had one talent. He couldn't condemn him for only having what the master gave him. Instead, he was upset the servant was lazy. Those given little can be as unfaithful as those given much. God might not expect a lot, but He expects something. His expectations might not be high, but He still has expectations.

In the parable of the sower, Jesus taught "some [produce] a hundredfold, some sixty, some thirty" (Matthew 13:23). Believers don't produce the same amount, but every believer produces some amount. People who claim to be Christians but aren't serving the Lord at all—they have no works—are deceived about their salvation.

Christians must serve the Lord, even if only in small ways. The two faithful servants had works, and they were invited into heaven.

The unfaithful servant had no works, and he was cast into hell. This looks as though they were saved by works. How do we explain this since we know "by grace [we] have been saved through faith, and that not of [ourselves]; it is the gift of God, *not of works*, lest anyone should boast" (Ephesians 2:8–9)?

We aren't saved by works, but they're the evidence of being saved. James 2:17 and 20 state, "Faith without works is dead." Saving faith is a living faith, and a living faith is a fruitful faith.

We're wrong if we think Ephesians 2:8–9 teach that we don't need to have good works in our lives. These might be the two most well-known verses in the Bible about salvation being by grace through faith apart from works, but the next verse says, "For we are His workmanship, created in Christ Jesus *for good works*, which God prepared beforehand that we should walk in them" (Ephesians 2:10). Laziness is such a serious sin because it's failing to walk in the good works God prepared for us.

Works are the evidence of salvation, because they reveal that we are "His workmanship," and that we are the fruitful servants who will be invited into heaven. Conversely, the lack of good works reveals the lazy servants who are not "His workmanship" and will be cast into hell.

Laziness Can Make People Wicked

Take your mind back to the investment manager who acted like the third servant. What would you call him? Lazy! Although, I doubt you would call him wicked. Typically, we think people are wicked because of what they do, such as commit murder, adultery, homosexuality, pedophilia, or rape. Surprisingly, the third servant was wicked, not because of what he did, but because of what he didn't do. He was lazy.

Some people haven't committed notoriously wicked sins, but if they've been lazy throughout their lives, they'll stand as condemned as people who committed notoriously wicked sins. They aren't wicked because of commission (sins they committed), but because of omission (not doing what God wanted). Failing to do what God wants is as serious as doing what God doesn't want us to do (stealing, lying, lusting). James 4:17 says, "Therefore, to him who knows to do good and does not do it, to him it is sin." None of us do all the good God wants us to do, but if we habitually fail to do the good God wants us to do, our behavior becomes wicked.

Distinguishing Between Faithful and Lazy Servants

The gospel of Matthew contains many contrasting pairs:

- Sheep versus wolves in sheep's clothing (Matthew 7:15–20)
- A house built on the rock versus a house built on sand (Matthew 7:24–27)
- Wheat versus tares (Matthew 13:24–30)
- A forgiven servant versus an unforgiving servant (Matthew 18:21–35)
- A wise servant versus an evil servant (Matthew 24:45–51)
- Foolish virgins versus wise virgins (Matthew 25:1–13)

The parable of the talents contains another contrasting pair: faithful servants versus a lazy servant. In each pair, the counterfeit looks like the genuine: wolves in sheep's clothing look like sheep, the house on sand looks like the house on the rock, and tares look like wheat. Just as the true identity of the house built on sand was revealed by the storms and the true identity of the foolish virgins was revealed when the door was shut, the lazy servant's true identity was revealed when he was judged.

John explains what was going on behind the scenes (1 John 2:19): "They went out from us, but they were not of us; for if they had been of us, they would have continued with us; but they went out that they might be made manifest, that none of them were of us." These people looked like Christians until "they went out." It was only them going out that revealed: "they were not of us." If they had not gone out, they would've looked saved until they stood before the Lord and faced the same judgment as the third servant. Many people claim to be Christians, and they can look like Christians at times, but if their lives are characterized by unfaithfulness, they are like the lazy servant.

Believers and Unbelievers Both Experience Extremes

All three servants experienced extremes. After the master rebuked the third servant, Matthew 25:29 records, "For to everyone who has, more will be given, and he will have abundance; but from him who does not have, even what he has will be taken away." Jesus said something almost identical in Matthew 13:12. As mentioned earlier, God is repetitive when He wants to make sure we don't miss something. God wants us to learn that if we're faithful, we'll receive more responsibility, but if we're unfaithful, we'll lose what's been given to us.

I used to be an elementary school teacher, and at the beginning of each year, I distributed responsibilities so that each student received at least one: passing out papers, collecting papers, line leader, opening the door, or taking the lunch money to the office. As the year progressed, some students showed themselves to be faithful, while others showed themselves to be unfaithful. I had to take the responsibilities from unfaithful students and give them to faithful students who already had responsibilities. By the end of the year, some students had an "abundance," but for others, "what [they] had was] taken away from [them]."

Hebrews 5:11–12 records an example of people losing what was given to them because they didn't use it:

> Of [Jesus] we have much to say, and hard to explain, since you have become dull of hearing. For though by

this time you ought to be teachers, you need someone to *teach you again* the first principles of the oracles of God; and you have come to need milk and not solid food.

They were taught "the first principles," but because they didn't use them, they lost them and had to be taught again. The same happened with the lazy servant: He didn't use what God gave him, and it was taken from him.

Punishment upon Punishment for Unbelievers

Just as my unfaithful students lost what was given to them, and the Hebrew readers lost what was given to them, unfaithful servants lose what's given to them. The third servant's only talent was taken from him, and then he was cast into hell to experience unimaginable torment forever.

The "outer darkness" is furthest from the light. Since 1 John 1:5 says, "God is light and in Him is no darkness at all," the "outer darkness" is the furthest separation from God. "Weeping and gnashing of teeth" describes the unending torment of hell. The worst suffering we experience becomes more bearable when we consider that it will end. Hopelessness is the hell within hell because hell's inhabitants know the suffering never ends. For unbelievers, it's loss upon loss upon loss for all eternity.

Blessing upon Blessing for Believers

Just as the lazy servant lost everything, faithful servants gain everything. The first two servants were commended by the master and invited to share in His joy. They received talents from unprofitable servants. More was given to them until they had an abundance.

Just as I looked for faithful students, God looks for, and graciously equips, faithful servants. Just as I rewarded faithful students with greater responsibility, God rewards faithful servants with greater responsibility. Typically, we think the reward for hard work is a raise or extra vacation, but God rewards faithfulness with greater service to Him in the future.

The master told the first two servants, "I will make you ruler over many things." They were promoted. They went from being servants to rulers. Since they were "faithful over a few things," it would make sense for them to be rulers over "a few things," but the master said they would rule over "many things." God graciously rewards us beyond what we deserve. He is "able to do exceedingly abundantly above all that we ask or think" (Ephesians 3:20). As Christians, we inherit eternal life and immeasurable blessings upon blessings.

Equipped by God's Grace

How are we to understand God rewarding us without this producing pride and contradicting confidence in His grace? The abilities we have for obeying God are gifts from Him in the first place; therefore, we can't take credit! God is simply "crowning His own gifts," as Augustine wrote:

> The Lord, He says, will award me a crown, being a just judge. So He owes me what He will award; so the just Judge will award; having inspected the work, after all, He can't deny the reward...But with the reward you do nothing; with the work, you don't act alone. The crown simply comes to you from Him; the work on the other hand comes from you, but only with Him helping...To Paul fighting the good fight, completing the course, keeping the faith, He paid back good things. But for what good things? For ones He himself had given. Or wasn't it by His gift that you were able to fight the good fight? ...The only things of yours that we know were prepared for you by yourself are evil. So *when God crowns your merits, he is not crowning anything but His own gifts.*[iii]

Our faithfulness is a result of God creating us anew and then faithfully equipping us. In 2 Corinthians 9:8, Paul wrote, "God is able to make *all grace abound toward you*, that you, always having all sufficiency in all things, may have an *abundance for every good work.*" God doesn't call us to a task and then expect us to perform it in our own effort. He calls us to a task and gives us the grace we need to complete it. As has been said before, "God does not call the equipped. He equips the called." He is with us, providing for us, and enabling us.

Let Ephesians 2:10 be a foundational verse as you continue through this book, so you don't look to your own strength and become proud: "For we are His workmanship, created in Christ Jesus for good works, *which God prepared beforehand that we should walk in them.*" Since God's grace equips us to do what He "prepared beforehand" for us, there is no place for pride; however, there is the assurance that we have what we need regarding the works God wants us to "walk in." God's grace has the glorious effect of producing good works—never perfect or entirely free of pride—but enabled by Him for His glory.

Romans 8:32 says, "He who did not spare His own Son, but delivered Him up for us all, how shall He not with Him also freely give us all things?" Thinking on all God has done for us, and all He has in store for us, how can we not be motivated to work for God's glory and resist the temptation to be lazy? If this isn't enough, the Bible's teaching on laziness in the following chapter will help us work God's way!

Chapter Three

The Sluggard's Sobering Example

G od's Word provides the conviction that can help Christians resist laziness. Commit the verses in this chapter (or at least their locations in the Bible) to memory. The next time you're tempted to remain on the couch when there's work to do, or sleep in later than you should, review these passages.

The sluggard is characterized by inactivity and doesn't take responsibility for himself. He can work but refuses to do so. He lacks the drive, personal responsibility, and common sense to provide for his needs.

The sluggard is not a Christian who occasionally gives in to the temptation to be lazy. Instead, he is habitually lazy, and his life serves as evidence that he is unregenerate. He is mentioned fourteen times in Proverbs, and each instance condemns his behavior and warns of the consequences. There is nothing good said about him. Since he is dead in his sins, his laziness can't be corrected by mere information, even biblical information. He needs the transformation of regeneration to repent and change.

Proverbs is the book of wisdom, filled with practical teaching for daily living. Since Jesus "became for us wisdom from God" (1

Corinthians 1:30), all proverbs point to Him. In John 8:23, He said, "I am from above." James 3:17 says, "The wisdom that is from above is first pure, then peaceable, gentle, willing to yield, full of mercy and good fruits, without partiality and without hypocrisy." Jesus is the embodiment of the wisdom from above, and only in looking to Him in the Proverbs can the sluggard's life be remedied. As preacher and theologian, Charles Bridges, wrote:

> But with all care to preserve a soundly-disciplined interpretation, we must not forget, that the Book of Proverbs is a part of the volume entitled—"The word of Christ" (Colossians 3:16). And so accurately does the title describe the Book, that the study of it brings the whole substance of the volume before us. It furnishes indeed the stimulating motive to search the Old Testament Scripture [which testifies of Christ] (John 5:39)—the true key that opens the Divine Treasure-house—"If we do not see the golden thread through all the Bible, marking out Christ, we read the Scripture without the Key."[iv]

Learning from Ants

A proverb is a short saying that expresses a general truth for practical living. There are so many proverbs dealing with laziness it would take up too much room to cover all of them. We'll consider the three main passages (Proverbs 6:6–11, 24:30–34, 26:13–16) with other verses integrated.

> Go to the ant, you sluggard! Consider her ways and be wise, which, having no captain, overseer or ruler, provides her supplies in the summer, and gathers her food in the harvest (Proverbs 6:6–8).

The book of Proverbs is written as a wise father speaking to his son: "My son, hear the instruction of your father, and do not forsake the law of your mother" (Proverbs 1:8).[1] He tells his son to learn from the ant's example. She's a humble, industrious creature that works without anyone watching over her. We, too, should work without having someone standing over our shoulders. If you're a parent, you know the blessing it is when your children work without having to constantly tell them what to do.

Ants are also good examples of planning. They busy themselves storing food, so they're prepared for the winter ahead. Proverbs 30:25 says, "Ants are a people not strong, yet they prepare their food in the summer." Ants serve as a rebuke to lazy people who think only about the moment. Sluggards expect the benefits of labor without laboring, showing they don't understand the law of sowing and reaping. Since they don't plan, they don't have what they need to live.

Oversleeping—The Sluggard's Great Temptation

> How long will you slumber, O sluggard? When will
> you rise from your sleep? A little sleep, a little
> slumber, a little folding of the hands to sleep
> (Proverbs 6:9–10).

Oversleeping is one of the marks of sluggards. Asking "how long" implies this has been going on too long, and something bad is going to happen. For example, Exodus 10:3 says, "So Moses and Aaron came in to Pharaoh and said to him, 'Thus says the LORD God of the Hebrews: "How long will you refuse to humble yourself

---

[1] See also Proverbs 1:10, 1:15, 2:1, 3:1, 3:11, 3:21, 4:10, 4:20, 5:1, 5:20, 6:1, 6:3, 6:20, 7:1, 19:27, 23:15, 23:19, 23:26, 24:13, 24:21, 27:11, and 31:2.

before Me? Let My people go, that they may serve Me.""[2] The longer Pharaoh would not let the Hebrews go, the worse things became for him. The longer the sluggard sleeps, the worse things become for him.

All the sluggard knows is his tempting drowsiness. The two rhetorical questions, "How long will you slumber...When will you rise," are aimed at stirring him to get to work and ridiculing his preference to stay in bed. The three-fold repetition of "a little" shows the lazy person prefers "a little" more sleep rather than work.

He doesn't refuse to work. He simply won't get started. Newton's first law of motion states that an object in motion tends to remain in motion, and an object at rest tends to remain at rest. This law can apply to people too! Some people work hard, and they tend to stay in motion. Other people are lazy, and they tend to stay at rest. The poet Robert Frost said, "The world is full of willing people, some willing to work, the rest willing to let them."[v]

Physical Consequences to Oversleeping

If Scripture's condemnation of oversleeping isn't enough, science has found an increased risk of death from sleeping too long! There is a 30 percent increase in mortality rates for people who sleep more than eight or nine hours per night on average. In 2010, *The National Library of Medicine* published, "Sleep Duration and All-Cause Mortality: A Systematic Review and Meta-Analysis of Prospective Studies." The study found:

> Increasing evidence suggests an association between long duration of habitual sleep with adverse health outcomes. Long duration of sleep is a significant predictor of death in prospective population studies.[vi]

---

[2] See also Proverbs 1:22 and Psalm 74:10.

Poverty—The Sluggard's Payment

> So shall your poverty come on you like a prowler, and
> your need like an armed man (Proverbs 6:11).

Sluggards dream of the things they want to enjoy, but they won't work to earn them. Soon their dreams become nightmares. This is the first mention of a truth that is communicated throughout the book of Proverbs—laziness results in poverty:

- "Do not love sleep, lest you come to poverty" (Proverbs 20:13).
- "Poverty will come upon [the sluggard]" (Proverbs 24:34).
- "He who follows frivolity will have poverty enough" (Proverbs 28:19).

Lazy people deceive themselves. Since they don't expect the disaster that comes upon them, they aren't prepared. Two illustrations capture the suddenness and unexpectedness:

1. First, a prowler is a vagabond or drifter who silently creeps in and steals. Poverty surprises sluggards like thieves surprise people.
2. Second, the armed man is a bandit or a man with a shield. He forcibly imposes his will. Sluggards are overpowered and left in need.

Poverty is also caused by talk without labor: "In all labor there is profit, but idle chatter leads only to poverty" (Proverbs 14:23). Lazy people like to talk, but without work, they're like the second son in Jesus' parable:

> "But what do you think? A man had two sons, and he
> came to the first and said, 'Son, go, work today in my
> vineyard.' He answered and said, 'I will not,' but

afterward he regretted it and went. Then he came to
the second and said likewise. And he answered and
said, 'I [will] go, sir,' but he did not go" (Matthew
21:28–30).

Talk is cheap. It doesn't matter what we say. It matters what we
do. The second son was a lazy talker, but the first son was a
convicted worker.

Are Sluggards Funny?

Proverbs 26:13–16 describes lazy people with a can-you-top-this
quality that provides comic relief. This causes us to ask: Is laziness
funny? Not at all. Sluggards are the object of jokes in Scripture, but
although the verses are humorous, they are also very unflattering.
Reasonable people would want to ensure that these verses don't
apply to them.

Excuses—The Lazy Man's Strength

> The lazy man says, "There is a lion in the road! A
> fierce lion is in the streets!" (Proverbs 26:13).

Proverbs 22:13 records an almost identical verse. Remember,
God repeats Himself when He wants to make sure we don't miss
something. What makes this proverb so important that it's worth
repeating? Lazy people are filled with excuses, even if they're absurd.
This would be like a person in our day saying, "A piano might fall
on my head, so I better not go to work." For most people, the
possibility of a piano falling on them is so remote it is laughable, and
certainly no reason to stay home in bed.

Billy Sunday said an excuse is "the skin of a reason stuffed with
a lie."[vii] People who are good at making excuses are rarely good at
much else. Proverbs 15:19 says, "The way of the lazy man is like a
hedge of thorns, but the way of the upright is a highway." Lazy

people find reasons why they can't make it to work (they're surrounded by thorns), but the righteous find ways to make it to work (it's an open highway). The weather is too cold for the lazy man, so he "will not plow because of winter" (Proverbs 20:4). Any flimsy reason is enough to prevent him from working. If we're honest, when we give in to the temptation to be lazy, our excuses are often equally lazy.

When one of my children was young and we asked her to do simple things, such as pick up her clothes or clean up a mess, she would say, "I'm too shy." This excuse has stuck around our house as a joke that Katie and I repeat when we don't want to do something our kids ask us to do. We hope this reminds them of how ridiculous their excuses sound when they don't want to work. The way our children sound to us might be the way we sound to God when we make excuses to avoid doing what He wants us to do.

Starvation—The Lazy Man's Payment

> As a door turns on its hinges, so does the lazy man on his bed. The lazy man buries his hand in the bowl; it wearies him to bring it back to his mouth (Proverbs 26:14–15).

These verses use parallelism to again mock the lazy person's love of sleep. They are attached to their beds, like doors are attached to hinges. Their only activity is turning in bed, as a door's only activity is turning on its hinges. They are no more likely to get out of bed and go to work than doors are to get off their hinges. Lots of motion, but nothing accomplished.

We say lazy people won't lift a hand to help, but this proverb brings it to another level; the lazy man won't even lift a hand to feed himself. Doing so exhausts him because even that is too difficult. He summons the strength to put his hand in the bowl, but it's too much work to bring it back to his mouth.

The sluggard may not have to worry about reaching for food for long, though, because the longer he lives so lazily, the less chance he'll have to find something to eat. The words of Proverbs 26:15 are repeated in Proverbs 19:24 so we don't miss that the greatest threat to lazy people—even greater than poverty—is starvation. The mockery makes a legitimate point: lazy people starve, and it's their fault. Our nation is so opulent that poor people rarely go without food; however, in the Old Testament, starvation was a real threat. If people chose to be lazy, they were choosing to starve.

The Selfishness of Laziness

People might ask, "Why do you care if people are lazy? Their behavior doesn't affect you." It doesn't? Since lazy people don't want to starve, how do they survive? They "beg during harvest" (Proverbs 20:4), expecting others to feed them. Part of the reason Scripture condemns laziness is because it negatively affects others.

When lazy people choose not to work, they're also choosing to consume what others produce without producing themselves. They sleep while others are working. Laziness is a sin of profound selfishness.

The Lazy Man's Pride

> The lazy man is wiser in his own eyes than seven men
> who can answer sensibly (Proverbs 26:16).

Surprisingly, lazy people have high opinions of themselves, with smug, unteachable, "know-it-all attitudes." They don't help the real world because they live in a fantasy world. Their deception is twofold:

1. They consider themselves wiser than a host of wise men. No matter how many reasonable arguments are presented, they persist in their conceit. This makes them hopeless,

because as Proverbs 26:12 says, "There is more hope for a fool than for a man wise in his own eyes."

2. They believe their own excuses. Perhaps they think they're clever because of all the work they're able to avoid.

A Better Motivation

We can be motivated by the sluggard's example and the danger of what will happen if we give in to the temptation to be lazy, but is there a better motivation? Yes, the gospel itself!

Following conversion, there's a new calling that God created us for and recreated us to accomplish. We become Christians when the Holy Spirit regenerates us. This new life in Christ brings with it new desires and motivations. The transforming power of the gospel gives us a vocation that allows us to joyfully serve God and our neighbor. It is not enabled by our willpower or resolve, fear of punishment or forfeiture of reward, or—worse yet—our salvation that we thought we had in Christ. Instead, it is motivated by God's gracious sanctification in our hearts, because "we are His workmanship, created in Christ Jesus for good works, which God prepared beforehand that we should walk in them" (Ephesians 2:10).

As we concentrate on the biblical theme of work, it is tempting to gradually shift away from the whole teaching of Scripture to the selective and legalistic. Imperatives (commands) in Scriptures must be grounded in the indicatives (truths) of the gospel. God calls us to live holy, disciplined, godly lives, but we're motivated to obedience, not by fear or appeals to self-help, but by the Holy Spirit's work. As John Calvin said:

> Justification and sanctification, gifts of grace, go together as if tied by an inseparable bond, so that if

35

anyone tries to separate them, he is, in a sense, tearing Christ to pieces. Sanctification doesn't just flow from justification, so that one produces the other. Both come from the same Source. Christ justifies no one whom He does not also sanctify. By virtue of our union with Christ, He bestows both gifts, the one never without the other.[viii]

Any call to resist laziness that isn't motivated by the gospel will become formulaic and consequently legalistic. It will either produce spiritual pride or despair. However, if we labor in the power of the gospel, then we can do so joyfully and thankfully, which is truly working God's way!

Chapter Four

The Dangers of Spiritual Laziness

When we hear the word "lazy," we might immediately think of an unemployed forty year old living in his parents' basement, or people on welfare who are capable of working. They're physically lazy, but what about spiritual laziness? We aren't sleeping in bed all day or standing on street corners asking for money, but are there other ways we're lazy, such as spiritually?

The following verses begin with another strong criticism of physical laziness, but they introduce a spiritual application that we're wise to consider:

> I went by the field of the lazy man, and by the
> vineyard of the man devoid of understanding; and
> there it was, all overgrown with thorns; its surface was
> covered with nettles; its stone wall was broken down.
> When I saw it, I considered it well; I looked on it and
> received instruction: a little sleep, a little slumber, a
> little folding of the hands to rest; so shall your poverty
> come like a prowler, and your need like an armed man
> (Proverbs 24:30–34).

The end of these verses is repeated from Proverbs 6:10–11. God wants to make sure we don't miss two points. First, there's a strong association between sleep and laziness. Second, unexpected disaster awaits the lazy.

The words "saw...considered...looked" reveal that the father studied the field owned by the lazy man who lacks sense (devoid of understanding), just as he earlier instructed his son to study the ant. Wise people learn by observation, and just as we can learn from good examples (the ant), we can also learn from bad examples (the lazy man).

The lazy man's neglect is evident by the shambles and overgrown weeds infesting his property. The dilapidated state leaves the owner without profit. The owner is responsible for the ruin of his own field, depicting the way lazy people ruin whatever they encounter. Proverbs 18:9 says, "He who is slothful in his work is a brother to (or is like) him who is a great destroyer." What exactly do lazy people destroy, or waste, besides fields they own? Two things: the talents God has given them and the time of people investing in them.

Lazy people do such a bad job "working" that whatever they do will have to be thrown out or done again. They're more work than help. A sluggard is painful as an employee; no boss wants an inefficient sluggard who won't get the job done. Proverbs 10:26 says, "As vinegar to the teeth and smoke to the eyes, so is the lazy man to those who send him." Vinegar in our mouths and smoke in our eyes isn't deadly, but it is annoying, just like a lazy employee.

A Field (or Life) Overgrown with Thorns and Weeds

Thorns appear in the sluggard's life like they appear in his field. In both cases, he's too lazy to remove them: "The way of the lazy man is like a hedge of thorns" (Proverbs 15:19).

A field representing a person's life is a common metaphor in Scripture. Jesus told the parable of the sower with the different soils (fields) representing different people (Matthew 13:1–9, 18–23).

Regarding the ways God used Paul and Apollos in people's lives, Paul said, "I planted, Apollos watered, but God gave the increase. For we are God's fellow workers; you are God's field" (1 Corinthians 3:6, 9). When God described the work His Word does in people's lives, He said:

> For as the rain comes down, and the snow from
> heaven, and do not return there, but water the earth,
> and make it bring forth and bud, that it may give seed
> to the sower and bread to the eater, so shall My word
> be that goes forth from My mouth (Isaiah 55:10–11).

The rain and snow represent the Word, and the ground (field) that produces represents people's lives:

> For the earth which drinks in the rain that often
> comes upon it, and bears herbs useful for those by
> whom it is cultivated, receives blessing from God; but
> if it bears thorns and briers, it is rejected and near to
> being cursed, whose end is to be burned (Hebrews
> 6:7–8).

These verses tie together Isaiah 55:10–11 and the lazy man's field in Proverbs 24:

- The rain in Hebrews 6:7 that brings forth "herbs" parallels the rain of Isaiah 55:10 that "[makes] it bring forth and bud."
- The field in Hebrews 6:8 that "bears thorns and briers, is rejected and burned" parallels the lazy man's field (and life) in Proverbs 24:30–34 that is "overgrown with thorns [and] covered with nettles."

Just as fields are revealed by what they produce, so are we revealed by what we produce. Jesus said, "Even so, every good tree bears good fruit, but a bad tree bears bad fruit. A good tree cannot bear bad fruit, nor can a bad tree bear good fruit. Every tree that does not bear good fruit is cut down and thrown into the fire. Therefore, by their fruits you will know them" (Matthew 7:17–20).

Don't Rest on Previous Labor

The author of Hebrews spoke strongly to his readers about being rejected and cursed. Then he followed that up with encouragement for those who were saved:

> But, beloved, we are confident of better things concerning you, yes, things that accompany salvation, though we speak in this manner. For God is not unjust to forget your work and labor of love which you have shown toward His name, in that you have ministered to the saints, and do minister (Hebrews 6:9–10).

The author is more optimistic about his readers—he expects "better things [from them]"—than those "whose end is to be burned" (Hebrews 6:8). They have worked, and he expected them to continue working. Their labor was love for the saints, and this served as evidence of, or "[accompanied their] salvation." He said God would remember their works, and this can be one of the greatest reasons to be faithful. When we're tempted to be lazy, thinking about the rewards that await us provides the motivation we need to keep going.

Even though the author expected his readers to continue working, he didn't want them resting on their previous efforts:

> And we desire that each one of you show the same diligence to the full assurance of hope until the end, that you *do not become lazy*, but imitate those who through faith and patience inherit the promises (Hebrews 6:11–12).

The words "imitate those [of] faith" reveal he's speaking spiritually, versus physically. He's not warning about physical laziness. He's warning against spiritual laziness. Many of these Hebrews probably worked extremely hard physically, but did they put forth that same effort spiritually in their relationships with the Lord? Similarly, the author may be revealing the laziness we're guiltiest of—spiritual instead of physical.

Laziness about Spiritual Disciplines

During Sunday school, when I taught on this topic, a man became convicted and raised his hand. He humbly shared that he had worked hard his whole life, and right when I began to think he was being prideful, he said, "But I regret how lazy I've been when it came to the spiritual disciplines."

We work hard all day and feel exhausted when evening rolls around. When we look back on how we spent our time and energy, how much was invested in our relationships with the Lord? We slack off, not at our workplace, but regarding spiritual disciplines. Prayer, church attendance, Bible study, Scripture memorization, and Christian fellowship don't receive the attention they should. Neglecting the spiritual is neglecting the Lord. He isn't the priority He should be in our lives.

Neglecting the spiritual also implies there isn't spiritual work to do. But there's always more to be done. Paul said we should be "always abounding in the work of the Lord" (1 Corinthians 15:58). God wouldn't use the word "always" unless there's always something spiritually profitable for us.

There are unbelievers who need to hear the gospel. Jesus said, "The harvest truly is great, but the laborers are few; therefore, pray the Lord of the harvest to send out laborers into His harvest" (Luke 10:2). We can labor, pray for those who labor, or pray God sends out people who labor. There are believers who need prayer and encouragement. Paul said, "Comfort each other and edify one another" (1 Thessalonians 5:11). Who might God have us reach out to through a phone call, email, or text message with something as simple as, "I just wanted to see how you're doing. Is there any way I can pray for you?"

Jesus said, "I must work the works of Him who sent Me while it is day; the night is coming when *no one can work*" (John 9:4). Our time to serve the Lord on this side of heaven is limited; therefore, we must take full advantage of it. Ecclesiastes 9:10 says, "Whatever your hand finds to do, *do it with your might*; for there is no work or device or knowledge or wisdom *in the grave where you are going.*" We must serve the Lord to the best of our ability as long as He allows. Anyone who wants to avoid spiritual laziness can easily find an answer to the question, "What can I do right now for God?" Since Jesus redeemed us, everything—including our time—belongs to Him.

Laziness about Temptation and Sin

Hebrews 12:4 says, "You have not yet resisted to bloodshed, striving against sin." Opposing sin is described as "[resisting] and striving." These are military terms indicating considerable effort. There is no room for laziness in this conflict.

The author of Hebrews told his readers they hadn't experienced persecution that cost them their lives. Since they were called to that, they needed to avoid fainting under the lesser suffering that striving against sin caused them. Simply put, since they were called to die for their faith, they needed to be willing to do the smaller work of resisting temptation.

We must be diligent against temptation, but sometimes we choose spiritual laziness. We buckle under the pressure and give in to sin. As Christians, we have a contest within ourselves: "fleshly lusts war against the soul" (1 Peter 2:11). Those who hope to persevere must exercise the utmost diligence.

Mental Laziness

To discourage mental laziness, 1 Peter 1:13 says, "Therefore gird up the loins *of your mind*, be sober, and rest your hope fully upon the grace that is to be brought to you at the revelation of Jesus Christ." When men in the early church needed to act quickly, they gathered up their robes and tucked them in their belts. A close equivalent today is, "Let's roll up our sleeves."

Since Peter referred to Jesus as "a lamb without blemish and without spot" a few verses later in verse 19, it's probable that he was borrowing from Passover. The Jews ate the meal in haste, ready to move (Exodus 12:11). Peter is applying this metaphorically to our minds. We need to get mentally ready for action and do whatever it takes to eliminate those thoughts that trip us up.

Being sober in this context doesn't have alcohol in view. Instead, it means not becoming intoxicated with the allurements of the world, controlling our thoughts, and exercising sound judgment. We should have clarity of mind, be morally decisive, and look at things earnestly.

Why mention the revelation (or Second Coming) of Jesus? When we center our minds on that reality and live in anticipation of it, we escape many worldly entanglements that encumber us and hinder our spiritual progress. We live in the future tense, which means our present actions and decisions are governed by our future hope. Just as an engaged couple makes plans considering the future wedding, so we make plans today considering seeing Jesus at His return.

Christians looking forward to Christ's return have greater reasons to obey Him and be good stewards. Let's contrast Abraham and Lot:

- Abraham looked forward to the heavenly city (Hebrews 11:10). He lived considering that reality; therefore, he had no interest in the world's real estate. By doing so, he brought blessing to his home.
- Lot was attracted to the city of Sodom (Genesis 13:10). He tasted the pleasures of the world in Egypt and wanted to continue enjoying them. By doing so, he brought judgment to his home.

The following verse also discourages mental laziness: "As obedient children, not conforming yourselves to the former lusts, as in your ignorance" (1 Peter 1:14). This contrasts our new nature with our old one. According to Ephesians 2:2, we were "sons of disobedience," but now Peter says we should be "obedient children." Genuine salvation results in obedience.[1]

Prior to salvation, our disobedience could be blamed on our "ignorance." The word "ignorant" has a negative connotation in English. If someone said you're ignorant, you might feel insulted. But Scripture calls people ignorant, and it's not a criticism.[2] It simply means they didn't know. We tend to think ignorance is the opposite of wisdom, but foolishness is the opposite of wisdom. Ignorant is the opposite of knowledgeable.

Before we were saved our ignorance produced indulgence. We lacked spiritual knowledge, which led to all manner of fleshly and worldly pursuits. At that time, we didn't know better, but after conversion, we receive new natures preventing any excuses.

---

[1] Romans 1:5 says, "Through Him we have received grace and apostleship *for obedience* to the faith among all nations for His name," and 1 Peter 1:2 says, "Elect according to the foreknowledge of God the Father, in sanctification of the Spirit, *for obedience* and sprinkling of the blood of Jesus Christ."

[2] For examples, see Romans 11:25, 1 Corinthians 12:1, 2 Corinthians 1:8, and 1 Thessalonians 4:13.

We were imitators of the world, "conforming [ourselves] to the former lusts." After conversion, we must "not be conformed to this world, but be transformed *by the renewing of [our minds]*" (Romans 12:2). We shouldn't pattern ourselves after the desires that controlled us when we were unsaved. Paul's reference to the mind reveals where this battle takes place. This leaves no place for mental laziness.

We need to break away from the sins we committed prior to conversion: "You should no longer walk as the rest of the Gentiles walk, in *the futility of their mind*...put off, concerning your former conduct, the old man which grows corrupt according to deceitful lusts, and *be renewed in the spirit of your mind*" (Ephesians 4:17, 22–23). The battle for spiritual transformation is fought in the mind. This is why mental laziness, as well as spiritual laziness, is so dangerous.

Hopefully, from now on when we hear the word "lazy," we won't think only physically. The spiritual laziness we discussed in this chapter is as devastating as any physical laziness we might imagine. What is the solution to laziness, whether it's physical, spiritual, or mental? Diligence! We put off laziness of any sort and put on gospel-motivated, grace-enabled diligence, as we'll learn in the next chapter.

Chapter Five

The Importance of Diligence

Maybe you're reading this book because you want to be more diligent, repent of laziness, find joy in work, learn to rest, or all of the above. Changing is hard. As a pastor, I've heard many people say, "I'm going to stop this" or "I'm going to start that." I've said the same myself.

Only 64 percent of New Year's resolutions last longer than the first month, and only 46 percent last longer than six months.[ix] We often begin well, but within a short period of time, we find ourselves resuming what we committed to stopping or stopping what we committed to starting. How can we change...*for good?*

Apply the Principle of Putting Off and Putting On

The single greatest reason we fail to change, at least regarding sin, is we "put off" without "putting on." When we hear the word "repent," unfortunately we often think only of stopping, but we must also think of starting. If there's a sin we want to repent of, we must replace it with a corresponding behavior.

John the Baptist is a man whose message can be summarized in the word "repent." He said, "Bear fruit in keeping with repentance"

(Matthew 3:8 and Luke 3:8). We don't typically associate repentance (stopping) with bearing fruit (starting), but we should. The apostle Paul also knew how to preach repentance. In Acts 26:20 he said, "Repent, turn to God (stopping), and do works befitting repentance (starting)."

This is known as putting off and putting on, or severing and replacing, and it's explained in Ephesians 4:

- Verse 25 says, "Put away lying." This is what we put off, followed by: "Let each one of you speak truth with his neighbor." This is what we put on. We can't simply stop lying. We must also make a conscious effort to start telling the truth; ensure what we say is accurate.

- Verse 28 says, "Let him who stole steal no longer." This is what we put off, followed by: "Rather let him labor, working with his hands what is good, that he may have something to give him who has need." We can't simply stop stealing. We must replace theft with hard work and generosity. Since this is a book about work's blessings, it's worth noticing that it serves as a remedy for theft!

- Verse 29 says, "Let no corrupt word proceed out of your mouth." This is what we put off, followed by: "But what is good for necessary edification, that it may impart grace to the hearers." We can't simply stop saying unwholesome things. We must intentionally speak words that edify and encourage.

Verse 31 sums it up: "Let all bitterness, wrath, anger, clamor, and evil speaking be put away from you, with all malice." Put off all this, and then put on verse 32: "Be kind to one another, tenderhearted, forgiving one another, even as God in Christ forgave you." Paul makes the same point in Colossians 3:

- Verse 8 says, "Now you are to put off all these: anger, wrath, malice, blasphemy, filthy language out of your mouth."
- Verses 12 and 13 say, "Put on tender mercies, kindness, humility, meekness, longsuffering, bearing with one another, and forgiving one another."

When we repent of the sins in verse 8, we'll produce the fruit in verse 12. The actions are presented in opposing pairs. If there's a sin that you need to repent of, but it is not mentioned in these verses, determine the opposite of that sin. More than likely that is what you need to put on.

Remember, stopping is only the first step. The second step is starting the accompanying behavior that fills the vacuum that was created. In the parable of the unclean spirit, Jesus described the danger of taking the first step (putting off) without taking the second (putting on). Matthew 12:43–45 records:

> When an unclean spirit goes out of a man, he goes through dry places, seeking rest, and finds none. Then [the unclean spirit] says, "I will return to my house from which I came." And when he comes, he finds it empty, swept, and put in order. Then he goes and takes with him seven other spirits more wicked than himself, and they enter and dwell there; and the last state of that man is worse than the first.

At first, things seem good because the unclean spirit (sin) is removed from the man's life. Unfortunately, he didn't fill the void, and as a result, his life (the house), remained empty. The man ended up worse off than when the unclean spirit left. This reveals the unfortunate human tendency for reform to be temporary. Psychologists, prisons, and juvenile centers testify to this. People will be sorry, stop for a little while, but soon find themselves doing the same thing again. Why? They fail to produce the necessary fruit.

In counseling, people who thought they repented will say "I stopped this. Why do I keep struggling?" My reply is, "You stopped, but what did you start? You put off, but what did you put on?" Let me give you some practical examples:

- You stopped going to bars, but what did you start doing?
- You stopped yelling at your kids, but what did you start saying to them?
- You stopped watching things you should not, but did you start reading your Bible more?
- You stopped coveting, but did you start giving?

When there's sin in your life, make sure your prayers are twofold. First, ask the Lord, "What do you want me to repent of and put off?" Then, "What accompanying fruit do you want me to produce and put on?"

Put on Diligence

The practice of putting off and putting on should be applied to multiple areas of the Christian life, including work and rest. Everyone struggles with laziness to some extent. If we're going to put it off, what should we put on? Diligence! Whether we're lazy physically, mentally, or spiritually, we need diligence! We put off whatever form of laziness we struggle with and commit to being diligent.

The Prodigal Son is a good example. His first request was, "Father, give me" (Luke 15:12). When he repented and returned home, his second request was, "Make me like one of your hired servants" (Luke 15:19). He put off the lazy, entitled attitude that got him into trouble, and he put on the humble, diligent attitude of a servant. Back in Hebrews 6:11–12, the author said, "Show the same *diligence* to the full assurance of hope until the end, that you do not become *lazy*." If they were going to persevere, they needed to put off laziness and put on diligence.

What is diligence? According to Dictionary.com, diligence is "constant and earnest effort to accomplish what is undertaken; persistent exertion of body or mind."ˣ Diligent people get the job done. They don't quit until they have completed the job. The Bible uses the word "diligence" in several ways, and just as sluggard is always used negatively, diligence is always used positively.

Although the words "put off" and "put on" are not used in the book of Proverbs, there are repeated demonstrations of this principle by the discussion of these pairs:

- Wisdom versus foolishness
- Patience versus hastiness
- Pride versus humility
- Truth versus deceit
- Obedience versus disobedience
- Righteousness versus unrighteousness

Proverbs encourages putting off laziness and putting on diligence by frequently coupling them together.

An Important Point

The book of Proverbs contains life principles that are generally true, but they're not guarantees. This must be understood before digging into the verses because of the health and wealth preachers who distort the gospel.

They misuse proverbs to teach that God wants people to become rich, be promoted, and never lose a job, but the following verses don't make these promises. Instead, they commend hard work and condemn laziness. They encourage the diligent and warn the slothful.

The Diligent Accumulate Wealth

> He who has a slack hand becomes poor, but the hand of the diligent makes rich. He who gathers in summer is a wise son; he who sleeps in harvest is a son who causes shame (Proverbs 10:4–5).

There's a clear cause-and-effect relationship between diligence and its rewards, and laziness and its heartbreaking consequences. It pays, literally, to be diligent; they reap wealth as their reward. The lazy have only themselves to blame, and they reap the consequences of their actions: poverty. A "slack handed person" slacks off at work, or slacks off in looking for work. When people don't have a job, their full-time job is looking for work. Warren Wiersbe said: "A new college graduate was asked if he was looking for work. He thought for a minute and then replied, 'No, but I would like to have a job.' That seems to be the attitude of too many people today."[xi]

Just as laziness and diligence are contrasted, so are work (gathers in summer) and sleep. Just as ants store food for the winter ahead, so do the diligent prepare for the future: "He who tills his land will have plenty of bread" (Proverbs 12:11 and 28:19). This is repeated to make the point that work allows people to eat. Diligence is manifested in the foresight to store up food in the summer rather than sleep through the harvest. Just as lazy people sleep while the ant works, they also sleep while the diligent work.

Why mention sons? Diligent children bless their parents. Conversely, lazy children "[cause] shame." The writer of Proverbs is repeating for emphasis: laziness affects others, and the people most affected are often the parents. Think of elderly people providing for their grown children. They're forced to care for children who should be caring for them. This is shameful.

This also looks beyond agriculture to laying hold of life's opportunities. Lazy people, like everyone, receive opportunities;

however, they don't take advantage of them, or they're unprepared to seize them when they arise. While the lazy are busy turning over in bed, diligent people are taking the openings God gives them.

We tend to think the richest are the most fortunate, just as we tend to think the most successful are the most talented. While some amount of fortune and talent come into play, diligence is the key difference. Two great inventors attributed their success to their effort. Thomas Edison said, "I never did anything worth doing by accident, nor did any of my inventions come by accident; they came by work."[xii] Benjamin Franklin, wrote, "Diligence is the mother of good luck, and God gives all things to industry."[xiii] These men, and others like them, succeeded because they were diligent. What about the scientific discoveries that seem to occur by accident? Perhaps that was the case, but there was considerable diligence leading up to the breakthrough.

The Diligent Are Promoted

> The hand of the diligent will rule, but the lazy man
> will be put to forced labor (Proverbs 12:24).

Whether the Egyptians with the Israelites, the Israelites with the Canaanites, or the Babylonians with the Jews, forced labor is always presented negatively in Scripture (Exodus 1:11, Judges 1:28, Lamentations 1:1). People who are forced to labor for others are not serving freely. They're slaves.

Lazy people shouldn't expect to rule: "[Wisdom] will promote you," but "shame shall be the promotion of fools" (Proverbs 4:8, Proverbs 3:35 KJV). Wisdom leads to promotion, and it's manifested through diligence. The "promotion" of fools is shame, and it's manifested through laziness. The lazy become slaves to the diligent because the diligent are promoted, and the lazy have no choice but to serve them.

While borrowing isn't always a consequence of laziness, sometimes it is. When the lazy borrow, they become slaves: "The rich rules over the poor, and the borrower is servant to the lender" (Proverbs 22:7). The lazy are forced to work off what they owe (see Leviticus 25:39–55 and Deuteronomy 15:12–18), and they serve the diligent. Ironically, lazy people seek to avoid work, but they lose their freedom and find themselves in bondage. Their lives of sleep and leisure result in lives of menial, undesirable labor.

While the lazy are "put to forced labor," the diligent attain authority and independence for their work. Diligence pays in more ways than just money! It also produces character that others can trust. Rare is the employer who doesn't notice a diligent employee. His "hand will rule" as he receives promotions, raises, and greater responsibility. We learned in the parable of the talents that this is how the master rewards diligence: "You were faithful over a few things; I will make you ruler of many things" (Matthew 25:21). In the similar parable in Luke 19:16–19, the diligent servants were given authority over cities.

During college, I went through Army ROTC and then served as an officer. There was a common saying in the military: "You can't keep a good soldier down." In other words, the diligent will be promoted. Allen Ross said, "The diligent rise to the top and the lazy sink to the bottom."[xiv] Proverbs 22:29 says, "Do you see a man who excels in his work? He will stand before kings; he will not stand before unknown men."

Joseph was faithful in Pharaoh's house, and then he found himself over all Egypt. Joshua was faithful as Moses' servant, and then he found himself over the nation. Part of Psalm 78:70–72 records:

> [God] chose David His servant, and took him from
> the sheepfolds; to shepherd Jacob His people, so he
> shepherded them according to the integrity of his

heart, and guided them by the skillfulness of his
hands.

David was faithful over his sheep, and then he found himself
over all Israel. His diligence was predicated on God choosing him
and making him the shepherd of His people, Israel. David was
faithful because he was chosen by God. He's a good example of
what we discussed in Chapter Two—God equips those He calls.

Isn't Jesus the premier example of diligence leading to
promotion? The author of Hebrews writes, "Consider the Apostle
and High Priest of our confession, Christ Jesus, who was faithful to
Him who appointed Him, as Moses also was faithful in all His
house. For this One has been counted worthy of more glory than
Moses" (Hebrews 3:1–3). Moses was faithful, but Jesus more so;
therefore, His promotion is greater (counted worthy of more glory).

We must "consider" Jesus because His perfect faithfulness and
obedience enables our all-too-imperfect work. We want to be
diligent, but we're wrong if we think the solution is simply trying
harder. Instead, we must focus on the faithfulness of Jesus for both
our justification and sanctification.

The Diligent Finish What They Begin

> The lazy man does not roast what he took in hunting,
> but diligence is man's precious possession (Proverbs
> 12:27).

The wise father says nothing is more important (precious) than
diligence. Why such a strong commendation?

Without diligence, even what is valuable becomes worthless.
When lazy people are fortunate enough to catch an animal, the food
is lost, because they're too lazy to prepare it. The solution for them
is to be diligent and follow through to the end: "The end of a thing
is better than its beginning" (Ecclesiastes 7:8). Just as they won't
bring their hand to their mouth, they won't cook the food they

caught. In both situations, they won't be able to eat the food even though it's before them.

The Diligent Are Satisfied

> The soul of a lazy man desires, and has nothing; but the soul of the diligent shall be made rich (Proverbs 13:4).

This verse looks beyond money to cravings of any kind. The diligent plan, save, and work, which allows them to have their desires (soul) satisfied (made rich). Their cravings are fulfilled because they acted.

In contrast, the lazy never have enough; their desires are unfulfilled. Proverbs 21:25 repeats the theme of laziness leading to lack: "The desire of the lazy man kills him, for his hands refuse to labor." Lazy people have cravings too, but they remain unsatisfied because they're too lazy to do anything about them.

A Diligent Heart

A good night's sleep is one of the blessings of a diligent life: "The sleep of a laboring man is sweet" (Ecclesiastes 5:12). Diligent people sleep well because they worked hard all day, but is there another reason? God gave us consciences to convict us of sin. When we give in to the temptation to be lazy our consciences keep us awake, because we've been unfaithful with the precious time God has given us. Although, when we're faithful we can sleep well because we know we've been good stewards.

How can we ensure we put off laziness and put on diligence? Proverbs 4:23 says, "Keep your heart with all diligence, for out of it spring the issues of life." Everything we do flows from our heart; therefore, it must be protected. We must intentionally guard it, versus passively allowing anything and everything to enter it. David provided an example when he said, "I will set nothing wicked before my eyes" (Psalm 101:3). Picturing soldiers securing a base gives the imagery of what to do with our hearts.

Why are our hearts so important? The outward reflects the inward. Diligent hearts produce diligent lives. When we cultivate the internal through external spiritual disciplines—such as prayer, Bible study, and fellowship—the rest of our behaviors are affected. Then we can experience the blessings of a diligent life. Even more importantly, we can have fellowship with Christ Himself. Spiritual disciplines are not merely a means to diligent outcomes. Instead, we engage in them to "grow in the grace and knowledge of our Lord and Savior Jesus Christ" (2 Peter 3:18). Then our work flows from hearts that are in communion with Him.

Truly any diligence in our lives stems from Christ's diligence on our behalves. His work transforms our lives; therefore, the fruit we produce contributes to the glory of God because it is from God in Christ. Our sleep can be sweet, not because of anything we've done, but because of what Jesus has done for us.

Spiritual Diligence

Nowhere does Scripture present our relationships with the Lord in any sort of casual or lackadaisical way. Jesus said, "If anyone desires to come after Me, let him deny himself, and take up his cross daily, and follow Me" (Luke 9:23). Following Christ requires more diligence than any other area of our lives.

Unless we pursue the Lord with all diligence, we will fail. The world is too appealing, temptation is too strong, and distractions are too abundant. Jesus described what is needed: "'You shall love the LORD your God with all your heart, with all your soul, and with all your mind.' This is the first and great commandment" (Matthew 22:37–38). More important than anything else in life is diligently loving the Lord. If we do so, our actions will rightly flow from this pursuit. The grace of the gospel will work in our hearts and propel us toward godliness and holiness in all areas of life, including work.

Change is hard. We considered why we usually fail: we put off without putting on. We all have behaviors we want to stop, temptations we want to avoid, and disciplines we want to cultivate. Diligence is the necessary ingredient to all the above. One of the biggest threats is idleness. In the next chapter we'll learn why idleness is so dangerous to our efforts, and why it prevents us from working God's way.

Chapter Six

The Sin of Idleness

When I was growing up, I became friends with a boy my age who lived in a trailer park. As we got to know each other, I noticed his parents were always home. I thought dads woke up and, on most days, went to work. Then they came home in the evening. That's what my dad did, as well as the other dads I knew. So, I projected that expectation on my friend's father and was surprised when this wasn't the case. One time he invited me into his parents' little trailer, and they were playing Nintendo. When we left, he told me, "That's what my parents do." Along with eating and sleeping, that seemed to be about all they did. I never even saw them outside. Since this was before I knew what welfare was, I wondered how they had money for living expenses.

What is our obligation toward the lazy? Many people affected by economic downturns or other unfortunate circumstances desire to work, but can't find employment. On the other side of the spectrum are those who have become generational welfare recipients, preferring to remain on the government dole. In 2 Thessalonians 3:6–15, Paul provides the necessary answers; therefore, we will consider this passage piece by piece throughout this chapter.

Withdrawing from the Idle

> But we command you, brethren, in the name of our
> Lord Jesus Christ, that you withdraw from every
> brother who walks disorderly and not according to the
> tradition which he received from us (2 Thessalonians
> 3:6).

The strong language "we command" carried Paul's apostolic authority behind it; therefore, this was a binding order instead of a suggestion or recommendation. The Greek word for "command" is *paraggello*, which is a military term meaning, "an order handed down from a superior officer."[xv] This is the second of four times Paul used the word (also in verse 4 and twice in verse 10), because he viewed the church as an army:

- In 2 Timothy 2:3–4, he said a Christian "must endure hardship as a good soldier of Jesus Christ...that he may please Him who enlisted him as a soldier."
- In Philippians 2:25 and Philemon 1:2, he called Epaphroditus and Archippus "fellow soldiers."
- In Ephesians 6:11–17, he commanded Christians to wear armor and carry a sword.

If soldiers do not obey orders, there can be no order. Unfortunately, some of the Thessalonians were "disorderly" as Paul says in verses 7 and 11. The Greek word for "disorderly" is *atakteō*, and it means, "out of ranks; often so of soldiers."[xvi] Other versions, such as the NIV and ESV, translate *atakteō* as "idle." Although there are subtle differences between laziness and idleness, the general meaning is "undisciplined slackness." Ecclesiastes 10:18 gives a graphic description of the results of both: "Because of laziness the building decays, and through idleness of hands the house leaks."

Laziness and idleness prevent the things that should be done from being done!

Idleness is the opposite of diligence. Paul said to "withdraw from" those habitually committing the sin, versus following "the tradition" received from him.[1] The tradition he's referring to was in his previous letter when he told them "to work with your own hands" (1 Thessalonians 4:11).

Idleness is often physical, but it can also be verbal. Jesus said, "I say to you that for every *idle word men may speak*, they will give account of it in the day of judgment" (Matthew 12:36). Paul charged his spiritual son, "O Timothy! Guard what was committed to your trust, avoiding the profane and *idle babblings* and contradictions of what is falsely called knowledge" (1 Timothy 6:20). Idle speech often comes from idle people who like to listen to themselves. It wastes people's

---

[1] Traditions require wisdom because sometimes Scripture presents them positively, but other times negatively:

- "Now I praise you, brethren, that you remember me in all things and keep the traditions just as I delivered them to you" (1 Corinthians 11:2).
- "Therefore, brethren, stand fast and hold the traditions which you were taught, whether by word or our epistle" (2 Thessalonians 2:15).

These verses present traditions positively, but Colossians 2:8 says, "Beware lest anyone cheat you through philosophy and empty deceit, according to the tradition of men, according to the basic principles of the world, and not according to Christ." In Mark 7, the religious leaders criticized Jesus because His disciples ate with unwashed hands. This wasn't a hygienic handwashing, but a ceremonial one that had no basis in Scripture. Five times (verses 3, 5, 8, 9, and 13) their handwashing is called "the tradition of the elders/men," or "your tradition." In Mark 7:6–12, Jesus rebuked them saying they were hypocrites and their traditions:

- [Taught] as doctrines the commandments of men (Mark 7:7)
- [Laid] aside the commandment of God (Mark 7:8)
- [Were kept to] reject the commandment of God (Mark 7:9)
- [Made] the word of God of no effect (Mark 7:13)

People in the early church could determine which traditions to follow by reading the Scriptures and obeying teaching from the apostles, such as Paul and Peter.

time and is unprofitable. Instead, we should strive to be so productive we don't have time for idle words.

A Good Example to Follow

> For you yourselves know how you ought to follow us, for we were not disorderly among you; nor did we eat anyone's bread free of charge, but worked with labor and toil night and day, that we might not be a burden to any of you, not because we do not have authority, but to make ourselves an example of how you should follow us (2 Thessalonians 3:7–9).

Paul and his companions were willing to work side jobs to provide for themselves. They did not approach the Thessalonians to take their food or money, but to share Christ with them. As an apostle, Paul had the authority to receive financial support, but he gave up this right. He chose instead to meet his own needs and the needs of others.

In his first letter he said, "For you remember, brethren, our labor and toil; for laboring night and day, that we might not be a burden to any of you, we preached to you the gospel of God" (1 Thessalonians 2:9). This lightened the financial load on the infant church. In every city, there were itinerant teachers trying to get as much money as possible from the people, and Paul didn't want to be classified with them. His example silenced any accusers who might say he was in it for the money. As he wrote in 1 Corinthians 9:18 (ESV), he wanted to "present the gospel free of charge," so money wouldn't be a hindrance.

While church leaders have the right to set aside financial support as Paul did, his example is descriptive versus prescriptive. Elsewhere Paul wrote that church leaders have the right to receive support from the congregations they serve (1 Corinthians 9:7–14, Galatians 6:6, 1 Timothy 5:17–18) and Jesus demonstrated the same principle when He sent out The Twelve and then The Seventy (Matthew 10:9–10, Luke 10:7).

Since Paul was a good example of everything he preached, he said "you ought to follow us" (verse 7) and "you should follow us" (verse 9). He repeatedly told believers to imitate him (1 Thessalonians 1:6, 1 Corinthians 4:16, and Ephesians 5:1). Although it seems odd to follow or imitate the character of anyone other than Christ, in 1 Corinthians 11:1 Paul said, "Imitate me, just as I also imitate Christ." Since Paul imitated Christ, telling others to imitate him was indirectly telling people to imitate Christ. Not everyone is called to labor for the gospel free of charge as Paul did, but he can be imitated in most other ways.

There's application for church leaders because Christians look at their examples. Warren Wiersbe said, "Leaders may appeal to the authority of the word, but if they cannot point also to their own examples of obedience, their people will not listen."[xvii] Leaders gain authority from their positions, but they gain stature through godly living and sacrifice. Stature comes with time and earns leaders the right to exercise their authority.

There's also application beyond church leaders because all Christians should see themselves as examples. Adults, especially parents, should see themselves as examples because children imitate them. Children should see themselves as examples because they imitate and influence each other.

When Giving Does More Harm than Good

> For even when we were with you, we commanded you this: If anyone will not work, neither shall he eat (2 Thessalonians 3:10).

Acts 2:45 says the early church "sold their possessions and goods, and divided them among all, as anyone had need." The

Christians were happy to care for those who couldn't care for themselves; however, some took advantage of this generosity, became freeloaders, and lived off others' sacrifices. Paul attempted to combat this, not only by writing to them about work's importance in both of his letters, but the words "even when we were with you" reveal that he also communicated this in person.

Despite his efforts, some were still idle. Paul said they should go hungry because that can provide the necessary motivation to find employment. The best gift to give the idle is not food or money, but a job. If the idle are given charity, it can hinder the work God wants to do in their lives because they're prevented from experiencing the consequences of their actions. It is in their best interest to reach the low point that leads to repentance. The Prodigal Son demonstrates this in Luke 15:16–18:

> And he would gladly have filled his stomach with the pods that the swine ate, and *no one gave him anything.* "But when he came to himself, he said, 'How many of my father's hired servants have bread enough and to spare, and I perish with hunger! I will arise and go to my father, and will say to him, "Father, I have sinned against heaven and before you."'"

Anything that works against repentance is detrimental, including things that look loving, such as charity. How much damage would've been done if well-meaning people had "helped" the Prodigal Son? Some Christians disobey Paul's command (yes, again, he said, "we commanded you") and give to the idle. They defend their actions by saying something like, "If they don't use the money wisely, that's on them. I let God sort it out." No, it's not just on the idle person receiving the money. It's also on the person giving them the money because God commanded them not to do so.

What about people who are unable to work? Paul took them into consideration. He said, "will not work" to distinguish between those who are unable, versus those who are unwilling: "the lazy man's hands *refuse to labor*" (Proverbs 21:25).

A Better Approach to Charity

Our government gives people handouts that require little more than standing in line or walking to a mailbox to collect a check. The welfare system in the Mosaic Law was much different than ours. Farmers were told, "When you reap the harvest of your land, you shall not wholly reap the corners of your field when you reap, nor shall you gather any gleaning from your harvest. You shall leave them for the poor and for the stranger: I am the LORD your God" (Leviticus 23:22).[2]

This approach is better for two reasons. First, it provided for the poor by encouraging those who were capable of being productive to also be generous. This stands in contrast to the redistribution of wealth by taking from those with more to give to those with less as some in our nation promote. Second, it required effort from the poor. God did not tell farmers to harvest everything and then give to the poor. Instead, He told farmers to leave enough for the poor to gather themselves. Work gives people a sense of purpose, productivity, and dignity, which is why involving the poor in the process was to their benefit.

Ruth shows the beauty of this approach. She said to Naomi, "Please let me go to the field, and glean heads of grain after him in whose sight I may find favor" (Ruth 2:2). She could have said, "I'm with my mother-in-law, and we're both childless widows. We're the pictures of weakness and vulnerability, so everyone should feel sorry for us and give us handouts." Instead, she went to the field and gathered an ephah of barley, which is about twenty-six quarts (Ruth 2:17). Her example is a strong rebuke to lazy people.

---

[2] See also Leviticus 19:9 and Deuteronomy 24:19.

Work Keeps Us out of Trouble

> For we hear that there are some who walk among you in a disorderly manner, not working at all, but are busybodies. Now those who are such we command and exhort through our Lord Jesus Christ that they work in quietness and eat their own bread (2 Thessalonians 3:11–12).

Idleness breeds compromise; it is a foundation for other sins. When people don't work, they often find unprofitable, damaging ways to spend their time and energy. Some of the Thessalonians became "busybodies."

Apparently, the Thessalonians hadn't learned, because Paul already wrote something similar to them in his first letter: "mind your own business, and work with your own hands" (1 Thessalonians 4:11). If they worked hard, they wouldn't be able to mind anyone else's business.

First Timothy 5:13 says something similar: "They learn to be idle, wandering about from house to house, and not only idle but also gossips and busybodies, saying things which they ought not." They weren't busy working, so they became gossips who were busy with others' affairs. Work is the solution for nosiness.

Knowing this, Paul says "we command" for the fourth time (previously in verses 4, 6, and 10), and he adds an exhortation that involves two parts. First, work in quietness instead of causing division and disruptions. Second, eat their own bread that is earned from working, versus received from charity.

Work is Paul's remedy. They should put off laziness and put on diligence. If they settle down and begin orderly, hardworking lives, they'll be pulled away from the sins they're committing.

As an elementary schoolteacher prior to becoming a pastor, I can tell you—as can other teachers—that the best way to manage students' behavior is by keeping them busy. When students are working, they don't have the time to get into trouble. The same is often true with adults. If Adam and Eve performed the work God gave them, they might have been too busy to worry about the tree He told them to stay away from. Charles Spurgeon said, "A man who wastes his time in sloth offers himself to be a target for the devil, who is an awfully good rifleman. In other words, idle men tempt the devil to tempt them."[xviii]

David's Tragic Example

Before David became king, he was the picture of diligence. He spent his life working, fighting, and serving. He was a shepherd, psalmist, soldier, armorbearer, and general. He did so much that it seems as though he lived the lives of many men. Sadly, after becoming king, he gave in to the temptation to be lazy, and the most heartbreaking event of his life took place:

> It happened in the spring of the year, at the time when kings go out to battle, that David sent Joab and his servants with him, and all Israel; and they destroyed the people of Ammon and besieged Rabbah. But David remained at Jerusalem. Then it happened one evening that David arose from his bed and walked on the roof of the king's house. And from the roof he saw a woman bathing, and the woman was very beautiful to behold (2 Samuel 11:1–2).

Most of this is worded as a criticism of David. He should have:

- Accompanied his men to battle like other kings
- Went to bed in the evening, tired from a day well-spent, versus sleeping all day and rising in the evening
- Ripped his eyes away from the woman he saw

His tragic example combines compromise in many areas previously deliberated: sleeping too much (physical laziness), mental laziness, and spiritual laziness against temptation. Had David been with his men, his devastating sins of adultery and murder which followed would not have taken place. When we give in to the temptation to be idle, rarely do the consequences rival those David experienced; however, there are still consequences.

Working When Others are Idle

> But as for you, brethren, do not grow weary in doing good (2 Thessalonians 3:13).

Paul told the Thessalonians to "[do] good" (also in Galatians 6:9), versus simply, "work hard," because they had to be encouraged to continue being charitable. They shouldn't neglect the genuinely needy just because some were being lazy. Similarly, we shouldn't become cynical and stop giving, simply because some try to take advantage of our generosity.

They had to be told "not [to] grow weary" because they were tired of supporting lazy people. It's discouraging when you're working, but others are idle. You're tempted to think, "Why even bother when they're not doing anything?"

Our kids have trouble working, but it's made even worse when they think their siblings aren't working. One of the most common complaints Katie and I hear is, "So-and-so isn't helping." Just like it's discouraging for children, it's also discouraging for adults; therefore, Paul tells them: "Keep doing what you're doing! Don't stop being faithful because others are being unfaithful."

God's Solution to Elijah's (and Our) Weariness
The prophet Elijah could've benefited from Paul's counsel. He reached a low point in his life when he thought he was the only faithful prophet. First Kings 19:4 says he "went a day's journey into the wilderness, and came and sat down under a broom tree. And he prayed that he might die, and said, 'It is enough! Now, Lord, take my life, for I am no better than my fathers!'"

Twice God asked, "What are you doing here, Elijah?" (1 Kings 19:9 and 13). God could've added, "Versus being out doing what I want you doing?"

Twice Elijah gave the same reason for his depression in 1 Kings 19:10 and 14: "I have been very jealous for the LORD, the God of hosts. For the people of Israel have forsaken your covenant, thrown down your altars, and killed your prophets with the sword, and I, even I only, am left, and they seek my life, to take it away." Much of Elijah's depression came from thinking he was the only one serving the LORD. God told him:

> "Go, return on your way to the Wilderness of Damascus; and when you arrive, anoint Hazael as king over Syria. Also you shall anoint Jehu the son of Nimshi as king over Israel. And Elisha the son of Shaphat of Abel Meholah you shall anoint as prophet in your place. Yet I have reserved seven thousand in Israel, all whose knees have not bowed to Baal, and every mouth that has not kissed him" (1 Kings 19:15–16, 18).

God told Elijah two things. First, He said, "Get back to work." Head back out and perform three tasks: anoint Hazael, Jehu, and Elisha. Work is a good remedy for depression. Sadly, when some people are depressed, they remain in bed. They don't want to face the day. Typically, this worsens their depression, which makes further idleness even more likely. It's a downward spiral: depression begets idleness, which begets worse depression, which begets more idleness.

When people experience clinical, physiological depression, they typically have no control over their mental illness and must seek outside help. Although, when people's depression is a symptom of their behavior, often, the best thing they can do to improve is to get up and get busy with something productive.

Second, God said, "You're not serving alone." There were seven thousand faithful prophets in Israel. As discouraging as it is when others aren't working, it's equally encouraging when others are working. You start to tire, but their example keeps you going.

Maybe we say, "I, even I only, am left [working]." No matter how much we might feel like Elijah, we should be reminded that there's always at least a remnant of others being faithful too.

Shaming the Idle

> And if anyone does not obey our word in this epistle, note that person and do not keep company with him, that he may be ashamed (2 Thessalonians 3:14).

Laziness and idleness are so serious that when people call themselves Christians but commit these sins, we're to "note" them, so we do "not keep company with" them. Earlier in verse 6, Paul said something similar: "withdraw from every brother." These statements are synonymous with "Treating as a heathen and a tax collector" in Matthew 18:17 and "Purging out...not to keep company with...not even to eat with...putting away" in 1 Corinthians 5:7, 9, 11, and 13.

The Greek word for "keep company" is *synanamignymi*, and it only occurs three times in Scripture.[xix] The other two instances are in 1 Corinthians 5:9 and 11, which also discuss separation: "I wrote to you in my epistle *not to keep company with* sexually immoral people...I have written to you *not to keep company with* anyone named a brother...*not even to eat* with such a person." This is church discipline, which we typically associate with severe sins, such as sexual immorality, divisiveness, or theft, but in this account, Paul has idleness and laziness in view!

The idle who are unrepentant must lose the blessings that come from the body of Christ, such as fellowship, the ordinances (baptism and communion), corporate worship, service, and charity! For what purpose? So they "may be ashamed." They might not even think being idle, nosy, or a busybody is sinful. Keeping company with them communicates their behavior is acceptable. Separating from them can give them the knowledge their behavior is wrong. At that point, hopefully, their shame will lead to repentance.

Warning the Idle Versus Treating as an Enemy

> Yet do not count him as an enemy, but admonish him as a brother (2 Thessalonians 3:15).

How should we treat an unrepentant, idle person? If we encounter him, should we engage or turn the other way?[3] Paul gives a nice, concise answer: "admonish him as a brother," or "warn" as it's translated in the NIV and ESV.[4] The devil, the world, and the flesh are enemies to be defeated, but an idle person is an individual to be restored. A brotherly attitude can more easily allow for later restoration following repentance. Reaffirm your love for him, encourage him to repent, and remind him of the consequences of his sin: "We love you and hope you'll repent. We don't want to see you suffer any longer."

---

[3] As a pastor, one of the more common questions I receive is, "Should I seek out people under church discipline?" Matthew 18:17 says, "And if he refuses to hear [the two or three witnesses], tell it to the church. But if he refuses even to hear the church, let him be to you like a heathen and a tax collector." The words "if he refuses to hear the church," imply the church confronted him after they learned of the sin. This is when he's sought out. If he still won't repent, then he's viewed as "a heathen [or] tax collector," and is no longer pursued.

[4] This doesn't mean they are believers, but they might be and they're simply backslidden. The supplementary passage in 1 Corinthians 5:11 says, "I have written to you not to keep company with anyone *named a brother*." Notice Paul said, "named a brother" versus "is a brother." The NIV says, "claims to be a brother," the ESV says, "bears the name of brother," and the NASB says, "any so-called brother," to allow for them to be (or not be) believers.

At the same time, the usual fellowship isn't extended. Paul said, "[Do] not even eat with such a person" (1 Corinthians 5:11). It's all business. There's no chit-chatting, laughing, joking, or reminiscing. We're not rude, but we don't say, "How are you doing? How's work, life, and the kids?" Asking these questions diminishes the seriousness of the sin, because it gives the impression these topics deserve attention. They don't when contrasted with the main issue: unrepentant sin. An overly friendly conversation can lessen the likelihood of repentance by communicating their idle lifestyle is acceptable.

Understanding idleness is important for two reasons. First, so we know how to respond to the idle. Second, so we strive to avoid idleness, because we know it's opposed to God's will for our lives.

After reading a chapter about the dangers of idleness, we probably feel motivated to work, but what about when we don't feel motivated to work? What about when—speaking candidly—we hate our job? The following chapter will help us with the answer so we can work God's way.

Chapter Seven

When Work Feels Like a Curse

According to *Business Insider*, we spend an average of 90,000 hours, or about ten years, working.[xx] This is a long time, so hopefully, it's spent doing something we enjoy and find fulfilling. The reality is that even for people able to say they love their jobs, they still experience work-related trials. We know this because we live in a fallen world. The consequences of The Fall affect all areas of our lives, including our jobs.

Take your minds back to God's words to Adam:

> "Cursed is the ground for your sake; in toil you shall
> eat of it all the days of your life. Both thorns and
> thistles it shall bring forth for you, and you shall eat
> the herb of the field. In the sweat of your face you
> shall eat bread till you return to the ground, for out of
> it you were taken; for dust you are, and to dust you
> shall return" (Genesis 3:17–19).

I have written this chapter because of the curse. Hopefully, it will help you in those exasperating times when you feel the thorns and work doesn't seem like a blessing!

Baruch: A Man Who Hated His Job

Scripture contains a lesser-known account of a man who was fed up with his work, and that's Baruch, Jeremiah's faithful scribe. He's one of the unsung heroes of the Old Testament. Jeremiah was the most despised man of his day, and throughout much of his ministry, Baruch was his only friend. Jeremiah faced rejection and persecution from his countrymen. Being the closest person to Jeremiah meant Baruch experienced much of the same. At one point, Baruch started wanting something different for himself. Jeremiah 45:1–5 records:

> The word that Jeremiah the prophet spoke to Baruch the son of Neriah, when he had written these words in a book at the instruction of Jeremiah, in the fourth year of Jehoiakim the son of Josiah, king of Judah, saying, "Thus says the LORD, the God of Israel, to you, O Baruch: 'You said, "Woe is me now! For the LORD has added grief to my sorrow. I fainted in my sighing, and I find no rest."'
> "Thus you shall say to him, 'Thus says the LORD: "Behold, what I have built I will break down, and what I have planted I will pluck up, that is, this whole land. And *do you seek great things for yourself? Do not seek them*; for behold, I will bring adversity on all flesh," says the LORD. "But I will give your life to you as a prize in all places, wherever you go.""'

Baruch was discouraged. The words, "woe, grief, sorrow, [and] sighing" reveal he suffered mentally and emotionally. The words "fainted" and "find no rest" reveal he suffered physically. The words, "the LORD has added grief to my sorrow," reveal he suffered spiritually because he attributed his suffering to God.

How did God respond? Did He feel sorry for Baruch? Did He apologize to him? He said: "Do not seek [great things for yourself]." This is the opposite of the Prosperity Gospel, Health and Wealth Doctrine, or Name-It-and-Claim-It Movement, which teaches people to "Seek great things for [themselves]." In Joel Osteen's New York Times best-selling book, *Your Best Life Now: 7 Steps to Living at Your Full Potential*, he writes:

> God wants us to constantly be increasing, to be rising to new heights…God wants to increase you financially, by giving you promotions…God wants this to be the best time of your life. But if you are going to receive this favor, you must enlarge your vision. You can't go around thinking negative, defeated, limiting thoughts. If you will keep the right attitude, God will take all your disappointments, broken dreams, the hurts and pains, and He'll add up all the trouble and sorrow that's been inflicted on you, and He will pay you back with twice as much peace, joy, happiness, and success…God wants to give you your own house. God has a big dream for your life.[xxi]

If Baruch had Joel Osteen's theology, he'd be convinced that God wanted him to pursue something better for himself, but that couldn't have been further from the truth. *Your Best Life Now* was on the New York Times best-seller list for more than two years, and it has sold over eight million copies.[xxii] The book's popularity reveals how many people are deceived about what God wants for them.

We can learn from what God said to Baruch. He didn't want the scribe seeking these things for the same reasons He doesn't want us seeking certain things. As we consider what God said to Baruch, we find application for us.

There Might Be Things God Doesn't Want Us Seeking Because We Seek Them for Ourselves

As a pastor, I've told my congregation that they rarely come to me with easy, black-and-white questions. Instead, they ask me about challenging situations, such as, "Should I stay in my current job or look for another one?" I just concluded meeting with a couple who is considering adopting two children.

I experience enough difficulty counseling people in my church when I can speak face-to-face with them and hear all the details they want to share with me. How much more difficult—if not impossible—would it be for me to know what you, the reader, should do in your job when I don't have any familiarity with your situation? Therefore, let me be perfectly clear that I'm not encouraging you to get a new job or stay in your current one.

Maybe you're experiencing discomfort and distress, but God might be using it to grow you where you are, or He might be moving you on to something new. My desire is twofold: to help you make the right decision and to give you biblical encouragement for whatever job you're in.

God said Baruch wanted these things "for [himself]." Since most people couldn't read or write, being a scribe was a respected and lucrative profession. More than likely, he had high hopes for position, honor, and wealth. He knew if he didn't serve Jeremiah, he could've enjoyed a comfortable, and perhaps even, luxurious life.

Maybe you've felt this way at times? When determining whether to get a new job, our motivation is one of the most important considerations. Why might we want to leave our current job? Is it to seek great things for ourselves? Why are we upset in our current job? Is it because we think we aren't receiving great things for ourselves?

This life isn't about accumulating "great things" for ourselves. James 4:3 says, "You ask and do not receive, because you ask amiss, that you may spend it on your pleasures." This seemed to be the case with Baruch, and God rebuked him for it. If we want a new job, and our motives are selfish, we should expect God to view our motivation similarly.

In Matthew 6:33, Jesus said, "Seek first the Kingdom of God and His righteousness, and all these things shall be added to you." This is what we should seek! Notice Jesus said, "these things" versus "great things." If our highest motivation is God's glory and His kingdom, then we can trust God will give us what we need, whether it's a new job, or the grace to endure our current one. Either way, we must "seek first the Kingdom of God and His righteousness" versus "great things for [ourselves]."

There Might Be Things God Doesn't Want Us Seeking Because They Aren't Going to Last

God told Baruch He was going to "break down [what He] built, pluck up [what He] planted, [and] bring adversity on all flesh." God didn't want Baruch to seek great things because He was going to destroy everything. But He told Baruch, "I will give your life to you as a prize." Baruch wouldn't get all the "great things" he wanted, but he would get to survive. Many people were going to die in the judgment God brought, but he would be safe.

Baruch would take nothing with him, except for his life. The same is true for Christians in that we don't take anything with us when we die, but we receive eternal life.

Second Peter 3:10 says, "The day of the Lord will come as a thief in the night, in which the heavens will pass away with a great noise, and the elements will melt with fervent heat; both the earth and the works that are in it will be burned up." Even though we don't live in Jeremiah's day, Peter's words communicate the same truth to us that God communicated to Baruch. Similarly, in 2 Corinthians 4:18, Paul said, "The things which are seen are temporary," which is to say they're passing away. When Job lost everything, he said, "Naked I came from my mother's womb, and naked shall I return there" (Job 1:21). He encouraged himself with the reality that he came into this world with nothing and would leave with nothing.

Because of the temporary nature of this life, we shouldn't work for what it offers. Instead, we should work for the eternal. As Jesus said:

> Do not lay up for yourselves treasures on earth, where
> moth and rust destroy and where thieves break in and

> steal; but lay up for yourselves treasures in heaven,
> where neither moth nor rust destroys and where
> thieves do not break in and steal (Matthew 6:19–20).

We should work with heaven in mind, where the result of our labors will last for eternity. As C.T. Studd famously wrote in his poem, "Only one life, twill soon be past, only what's done for Christ will last."[xxiii] The question we should ask is: "How well does this job prepare me for eternity?" It would be better to work in a lower-paying, more-challenging job that is part of God's will than a high-paying, compromising job that is not God's will.

Focusing on eternity gives us the motivation we need on our worst days on the job. Ninety-thousand hours is a long time to work, but it's nothing compared with eternity. When we reach the end of our lives, we will be thankful if we were faithful in our work. This is the perspective that allows us to persevere when we're suffering in the workplace.

There Might Be Things God Doesn't Want Us Seeking Because They Aren't Part of God's Plan

It's possible the things Baruch wanted weren't selfish or immoral. The "great things" might have been good and moral, such as getting married, having children, and experiencing a normal life. These are part of God's plan for most people, but they weren't part of God's plan for Baruch.

If Baruch was going to follow God's plan for his life, he was going to have to give up "great things" he wanted. If we're going to follow God's plan for our lives, we're going to have to give up some of the "great things" we want. If they aren't part of His plan, then He would say the same thing to us that He said to Baruch: "Do not seek them."

Because we have limited amounts of time and energy, saying "yes" to something means saying "no" to something else. Let me share an example from my life. In the first few years of teaching elementary school in Marysville, California, I also coached middle school and high school wrestling. When I moved to Lemoore, California, I was only able to coach the middle school because the high school had a successful coach who'd been inducted into the State Wrestling Hall of Fame. The program was extraordinarily successful, winning nineteen consecutive league championships, and the facilities were some of the best I'd ever seen.

You can imagine my excitement when the coach moved on to the collegiate level and talked to me about taking over the high school program for him. The difficulty was that this coincided with two other things in my life. First, I started getting more involved in my church, and second, Katie and I started talking about marriage. We wanted to put our family in God's hands and allow Him to give us children as He saw fit, which meant parenting could've followed nine months later.

The commitment was huge to follow such a successful coach. He built the program by investing his life in it. There was no way I could take over without doing the same. I had to choose between two directions: coaching high school wrestling or marrying Katie and pursuing ministry. There's nothing wrong with coaching wrestling—I had done it for years earlier—but I could tell it was no longer part of God's plan for my life. I had to trade coaching a top tier high school wrestling program, which to me, was a "great thing" for something that might not have looked great to others: serving in the church and having a family.

Being Jeremiah's scribe meant giving up great things Baruch wanted, even though they weren't selfish or sinful. Similarly, embracing the job God wants us doing might mean giving up great things we want, even if they aren't selfish or sinful. Although, if our greatest concern is doing what God wants, we can be encouraged. Despite how things might look in man's eyes, as we'll see in the next chapter, if we're obeying God, we're doing something great in His eyes.

Chapter Eight

Seeking Great Things in God's Eyes

Samuel, the prophet, was a godly man, but he made a mistake when he was sent to anoint David to replace Saul. Jesse's sons stood before him, and 1 Samuel 16:6–7 records:

> So it was, when they came, that he looked at Eliab and said, "Surely the Lord's anointed is before Him!" But the Lord said to Samuel, "Do not look at his appearance or at his physical stature, because I have refused him. For the Lord does not see as man sees; for man looks at the outward appearance, but the Lord looks at the heart."

When each son was rejected, "Samuel said to Jesse, 'Are all the young men here?' Then he said, 'There remains yet the youngest, and there he is, keeping the sheep'" (1 Samuel 16:11). God chose David, the son whose name Jesse didn't even use, and who wasn't even invited to the anointing. Why? God sees things differently than man sees them.

Consider Moses unleashing the plagues on Egypt, David killing Goliath, and Elijah defeating the prophets of Baal on Mount Carmel. God was pleased when these events took place, and they're some of our favorite accounts to read in Scripture. In that sense,

81

they look great in God's eyes and man's eyes. But this isn't the case with everything in the Bible. Some things that look great in God's eyes might look bad in man's eyes, such as service, humility, and forgiveness. Conversely, some things that look great in man's eyes are not great in God's eyes—at least when they become idols or are used sinfully—such as fame, riches, and power.

Baruch's situation is another example. He found his job unfulfilling and miserable. Being Jeremiah's scribe was unattractive and unglamorous to him. But in God's eyes, he was doing a great thing. He was writing the very words of Scripture and serving one of God's faithful prophets!

As we think about our work, the question is never, "How does this look to man?" The question is, "How does this look to God?" When we can answer the second question, we can correctly evaluate our job.

Let's consider some people who sought great things in God's eyes. Their examples can encourage us and help us rightly view our situations.

Moses Pursued Greatness in God's Eyes

> By faith Moses, when he was grown up, refused to be called the son of Pharaoh's daughter, choosing rather to be mistreated with the people of God than to enjoy the fleeting pleasures of sin. He considered the reproach of Christ greater wealth than the treasures of Egypt, for he was looking to the reward. By faith he left Egypt, not being afraid of the anger of the king, for he endured as seeing Him who is invisible (Hebrews 11:24–27).

Moses "[saw] Him who is invisible," referring to God. This doesn't make sense, does it? We can't see what's invisible. The beginning of the chapter says, "Faith is the assurance of things hoped for, the conviction of things not seen" (Hebrews 11:1). Faith is seeing what

82

is invisible, which means Moses' faith caused him to turn his back on Egypt and all it represented.

Moses' life was charted. He could have grown up in Pharaoh's house with luxury, fame, safety, and ease, but he rejected all of that for a life of mistreatment and oppression. Moses knew the "pleasures of sin" were "fleeting" and temporary, so he embraced "the reproach of Christ." He didn't know Jesus as we do, but in identifying with the suffering of Christ's people, the Hebrews, he identified with Christ Himself. He did what we discussed earlier and focused on the eternal, keeping his eyes on heaven and "looking to the reward." While Moses' actions must have looked foolish in man's eyes, he did a great thing in God's eyes.

picture of Christ

Jonathan Pursued Greatness in God's Eyes

We know David replaced Saul as king, but nobody expected this, including Saul's own son, Jonathan, who grew up expecting to be the next king. Saul failed as the king, but Jonathan was a godly man who wouldn't repeat his father's mistakes. He was ready to receive the throne and become the king his father never was and do the job his father should've done. But something happened. God said, "I want David to be king."

The great thing Jonathan spent his life looking forward to wasn't going to happen. He could've gotten angry with God. He had every reason to say, "Why are you treating me like this and punishing me for my dad's sins? I'm not like him. What did I do wrong? I've served You my whole life. I would do a better job." Jonathan also could've gotten angry with David: "Why should he be king? He was a shepherd. His father, Jesse, was a nobody. Why does he get to take the throne from me?" But if Jonathan hated David and was jealous of him, then he would've been just like his father. Instead:

> When [Jonathan] had finished speaking to Saul, the soul of Jonathan was knit to the soul of David, and Jonathan loved him as his own soul. Saul took him

> that day, and would not let him go home to his
> father's house anymore. Then Jonathan and David
> made a covenant, because he loved him as his own
> soul. And Jonathan took off the robe that was on him
> and gave it to David, with his armor, even to his
> sword and his bow and his belt...

> [Jonathan] said to [David], "Do not fear, for the hand
> of Saul my father shall not find you. You shall be king
> over Israel, and I shall be next to you. Even my father
> Saul knows that" (1 Samuel 18:1–3, 23:17).

I don't think it's too much to say that Jonathan experienced one of the biggest disappointments in Scripture. When you spend your life desiring something and then find out it's going to someone else, you're discouraged. Embracing God's will meant giving up the great thing Jonathan wanted his whole life. To his credit, not only did he accept God's will, he did everything he could to see it fulfilled.

Becoming the second king of Israel would've looked great in man's eyes, but Jonathan's actions probably looked bad because following others is typically frowned upon. As the saying goes, "Second place is first place's loser." But in supporting David, Jonathan was doing a great thing in God's eyes.

John the Baptist's example is similar. He had a large following. When Jesus' public ministry began, John's followers began following Jesus:

> [John's disciples] said to him, "Rabbi, He who was
> with you beyond the Jordan, to whom you have
> testified—behold, He is baptizing, and all are coming
> to Him!" John answered and said, "He who has the
> bride is the bridegroom; but the friend of the
> bridegroom, who stands and hears him, rejoices
> greatly because of the bridegroom's voice. Therefore
> this joy of mine is fulfilled. He must increase, but I
> must decrease" (John 3:26–30).

John the Baptist was to Jesus what Jonathan was to David. Jonathan knew that for David to increase, he had to decrease. John knew that for Jesus to increase, he had to decrease.

In deferring to Jesus, John's actions looked poor to man. We know that because his disciples warned him about what was happening. But John's actions were so great that Jesus said, "Truly, I say to you, among those born of women there has arisen no one greater than John the Baptist" (Matthew 11:11).

John and Jonathan did great things in God's eyes, because they fulfilled His roles for them. Similarly, regardless of what anyone might think about our jobs, the greatest thing we can do is fulfill the roles God has for us. This is the case even if the jobs are despised by man.

Despised Jobs that Please God

The Babylonians destroyed the temple when they conquered the Jews. They rebuilt the temple decades later when they returned to the land. Some of the Jews saw Solomon's temple before it was destroyed, went into exile in Babylon, lived through the exile, and returned to Jerusalem for the rebuilding. When they laid the foundation for the new temple, "Many of the priests and Levites and heads of the fathers' houses, old men who had seen the first temple, wept with a loud voice when the foundation of this temple was laid before their eyes" (Ezra 3:12). They wept because they thought the new temple wouldn't compare with the previous temple. God rebuked them with two questions He asked through the prophets:

- Haggai asked, "Who is left among you who saw this temple in its former glory? And how do you see it now? In comparison with it, is this not in your eyes as nothing? The glory of this latter temple shall be greater than the former" (Haggai 2:3, 9). The new temple was inferior to Solomon's temple in man's eyes, but in God's eyes, it would be greater.

- Zechariah asked, "For who has despised the day of small things? For these seven rejoice to see the plumb line in the hand of Zerubbabel. They are the eyes of the Lord, which scan to and fro throughout the whole earth" (Zechariah 4:10).

The prophet wrote, "These seven...are the eyes of the Lord," but this doesn't mean God has seven eyes. Since seven is the number of completion this refers to God's omniscience, or complete knowledge, which allows Him to see "throughout the whole earth."

A "plumb line" is a builder's tool, and God "rejoiced" to see it in the hand of Zerubbabel, the Jews' leader. As the Jews rebuilt the temple, they "despised" it as a "day of small things," but in God's eyes, the work was great enough to cause Him to "rejoice."

This applies to us because we can despise our work and see it as days spent doing small things. Our jobs can seem insignificant, which might lead us to think God isn't pleased with what we're doing. If this happens, we should encourage ourselves with Zechariah's words to the Jews. God rejoices in the seemingly small things we do.

We shouldn't despise small things, because if they cause God to rejoice, then they aren't small things. They're great things because they please Him and bring Him joy. Great things are defined by God's pleasure.

Jesus said, "He who is faithful in *what is least* is faithful also *in much*" (Luke 16:10). Our faithfulness in little things is important because it reveals that we can be faithful "in much," or in great things. If we can't be faithful "in what is least," we won't suddenly become faithful if we're given more. When we give our children small tasks, if they don't do those well, we don't give them bigger tasks and expect them to do better. Likewise, when God, our Father, gives us, His children, tasks, He's looking for faithfulness in small, despised things before He'll entrust bigger tasks to us.

In the parable of the talents, the master commended the first two, "Well done, good and faithful servant; you were faithful over a *few things*, I will make you ruler over *many things*. Enter into the *joy of your lord*" (Matthew 25:21, 23). Similarly, in the parable of the minas, the master said, "Well done, good servant; because you were faithful in a *very little*, have authority over *ten cities*" (Luke 19:17). In both parables, the master didn't commend faithfulness over great things. Instead, He rewarded faithfulness over "very little" and "few things." These small areas of faithfulness might have been despised by the servants throughout their earthly lives, but this is exactly what pleased the master, brought him joy, and earned the servants rewards.

Living Quiet Lives

Paul said, "Aspire to lead a quiet life, to mind your own business" (1 Thessalonians 4:11). Instead of "seeking great things" and "despising days of small things," we should "aspire to lead [quiet lives]." The world tempts us to crave fame, attention, and recognition. Can you imagine anything less attractive in society's eyes than a quiet life?

What God wants from us is the opposite of what the world promotes. In God's eyes, little is more impressive than simple, humble, lives of obedience, often filled with small, ordinary routines. The days are far from glamorous. While this might sound discouraging, it should be encouraging, because it frees us from striving to become big, noticed, and heard.

First Corinthians 10:31 says, "Therefore, whether you eat or drink, or whatever you do, do all to the glory of God." Why did Paul mention eating and drinking? Because there aren't many "[smaller] things" than these! What could be simpler or more routine?

Colossians 3:17 says, "And whatever you do in word or deed, do all in the name of the Lord Jesus, giving thanks to God the Father through Him." Whatever we do, no matter how small or insignificant, can be done for God's glory and pleasure!

Most of Us Will Be a Thaddeus or a Baruch

The judges were important, but could most Christians tell you what they did? They could probably discuss Samson and Gideon, maybe Ehud and Othniel, but would they even remember the names of Tola, Jair, Elon, or Abdon?

Consider the kings. People could tell you about David and Solomon, maybe Hezekiah and Josiah, but would they remember anything about Amaziah and Jotham?

Consider the prophets. Most people know who Samuel, Elijah, and Jeremiah are, but do they know anything about Amos and Obadiah?

Consider the apostles, the most important men in the New Testament, second only to Jesus. If you ask people which apostle they most identify with, they'll probably tell you Peter. One reason is he was known for opening his mouth when he should've been quiet. Since James 3:2 says, "If anyone does not stumble in word, he is a perfect man, able also to bridle the whole body," most of us identify with Peter because we have the same problem. The other reason we can relate to Peter is there's so little written about the rest of the apostles that we can't identify with them!

Judas, the son of James, is also known as Thaddaeus to distinguish him from Judas Iscariot. He's mentioned in the lists of the disciples (Matthew 10:3, Mark 3:18, Luke 6:16, and Acts 1:13), and John 14:22 records, "Judas (not Iscariot) said to Him, 'Lord, how is it that You will manifest Yourself to us, and not to the world?'" (John 14:22). He's in the lists of the disciples, and he asks Jesus one question. That's all that's recorded about him.

Besides Peter, James, John, Judas, and Thomas (only because of the account of him doubting), what do we know about the other apostles? Ephesians 2:20 says the church is "built on the foundation of the apostles," and Revelation 21:14 says, "The wall of the [New Jerusalem] had twelve foundations, and on them were the twelve names of the twelve apostles." Could anything make the apostles sound more important? Yet most people couldn't name half of them.

I'm not criticizing people's Bible knowledge, but I am making a point: how famous are apostles, judges, kings, and prophets if people hardly know anything about them? Even the people in Scripture we tend to think were extraordinary were very ordinary. This should reassure us, because if we're going to "live quiet lives" filled with "small things," we're going to be more like Thaddaeus, Tola, Jair, Jotham, and Amos, than Peter, Gideon, David, and Elijah.

The Premier Example

As far as leading a quiet life and being faithful in small things, nobody modeled this better than Jesus. When you strip away the miraculous and supernatural, you see His life was characterized by modesty, humility, and simplicity. There was a lack of extravagance and glamor.

Why did the Jews reject Jesus? They thought the Messiah would deliver them from their oppression like Moses delivered Israel from Egypt. He'd be a great military leader like David—after all the Messiah was "the Son of David"—and give them victories over the Romans like David gave Israel victories over the Philistines. He'd be a great king and restore the nation to their Golden Age when they were wealthy and powerful like they experienced under Solomon. Instead, they had a Man walking around on dirt roads with "nowhere to lay his head" (Matthew 8:20). Jesus couldn't have looked less like a rich, glamorous king, and most of the time, He couldn't have lived a simpler, quieter life.

Moses, Jonathan, and John the Baptist's examples in humbling themselves are challenging, but how much greater is Jesus' example? Philippians 2:6–8 says:

> [Jesus] being in the form of God, did not consider it robbery to be equal with God, but made Himself of no reputation, taking the form of a bondservant, and coming in the likeness of men. And being found in appearance as a man, He humbled Himself and became obedient to the point of death, even the death of the cross.

Jesus could've lived like a king and experienced the best the world offers, but He was content to obey His Father and live a simple, modest life. In John 4:34, He said, "My food is to do the will of Him who sent Me, and to finish His work." His "food," or very existence, was a life of unassuming submission. This should be our food too. We find purpose in our work doing the will of God the Father.

At this point, we're encouraged to seek great things in God's eyes, which means living simple, quiet lives. But this introduces a question: What does that look like for each person? Surely it can't be the same for men, women, and children. So, in the following chapters we'll consider what it means for each person to work God's way.

Chapter Nine

Husbands Treat Their Wives Well by Working Hard

I've never met a man who wanted to be a bad husband, but I have met plenty of men who didn't know what it looked like to be good husbands. In 1 Peter 3:1, God commands, "Wives, likewise, be submissive to your own husbands, that even if some do not obey the word, they, without a word, may be won by the conduct of their wives." Then God instructs husbands regarding the treatment of their wives to prevent any abuses of the authority He has given them: "Husbands, likewise, dwell with them with understanding, giving honor to the wife, as to the weaker vessel, and as being heirs together of the grace of life, that your prayers may not be hindered" (1 Peter 3:7). This verse is packed with insight for husbands who want to be pleasing in God's eyes, and it begins by knowing their wives.

The Greek language has different words for "know" and "knowing." *Epistamai* means "to put one's attention on or to fix one's thoughts on."[xxiv] This is an intellectual knowledge that comes by perceiving or observing, but there is no personal relationship or experience. On the other hand, *ginosko* means "to learn, get a knowledge of, feel."xxv This is a knowledge that comes from a personal relationship or experience. For example:

- I know what rugby is even though I have never played it; therefore, I know it intellectually or *epistamai*. On the other hand, I have played football for years, which means I know it experientially or *ginosko*.
- I know of (*epistamai*) Abraham Lincoln historically, but I know (*ginosko*) my wife, Katie, relationally.

Husbands are told to "dwell with [their wives] with understanding," or knowledge of them, and the word for "understanding" is *gnosis*, related to the word *ginosko*. It describes such a close intimacy that the same word is used in Luke 1:34 when Mary said to the angel who told her she would give birth to the Messiah: "How can this be, since I do not know (*ginosko*) a man?"

Peter commands husbands to develop an intimate knowledge or understanding of their wives that comes through personal experience or relationship. Husbands must study their wives and learn them. Do wives want husbands who make "learning" them a priority? Definitely! Wives feel loved by being understood. A lot of wives wish their husbands knew as much about them as they know about sports, cars, television shows, friends, food, music, video games, you name it. What exactly are husbands supposed to know about their wives? What they like and what they don't like. What is important to them. What they desire and enjoy. A husband ought to know as much as there is to know about the woman he will live with for the rest of his life.

Any man who comes to know his wife well will soon learn that she wants a husband who works hard to care for her and their family. While husbands might tire of the routine—going to the same job day-after-day—this quiet, faithful life is a great thing in God's eyes, and a wife's eyes!

Wives Want Hardworking Husbands

Peter tells husbands to "dwell with [their wives] with understanding," and the word "dwell," or most translations say "live," communicates being together physically, but it means more than just occupying the same house. It refers to a husband making his wife his lifelong companion. Putting the words "dwell" and "understanding" together, the apostle Peter commands husbands to develop knowledge of their wives and then live with them according to that knowledge.

A husband should take what he has learned about his wife and apply that knowledge (or "understanding") to their daily lives together. He should understand how his wife feels loved and seek to treat her that way in their relationship.

Katie has given me permission to share two ways she appreciates me "[dwelling] with [her] with understanding" based on the knowledge I have of her:

1. Katie is a visionary, creative woman with lots of plans and thoughts. She likes to think months, years, or even decades down the road. On the other hand, I generally have one focus each week—making sure Sunday goes well. I count time by the number of days until the Lord's Day arrives. When Sunday is over, the countdown begins again. I rarely think eight days ahead (much less eight months or eight years). As a result, Katie appreciates it when I listen to her ideas no matter how far they are in the future, and regardless of whether there is much chance they will come to fruition.

2. Most strengths have a corresponding weakness, so even though Katie has lots of plans, she also has trouble finishing things she starts. Some of her favorite words to say to herself come from Ecclesiastes 7:8: "The end of a thing is

better than its beginning." In other words: Finishing is better than starting. Because Katie knows this about herself, she has asked me to do two things for her: encourage her to finish things she starts and discourage her from starting new things until previous things are completed.

These are simple ways Katie wants me to "dwell with [her] with understanding." Each wife is different, which means each husband must learn his own wife. While this might not be easy, God commands it, which means it is something every husband can and should do. Men should keep in mind that as much as wives are commanded to submit to their husbands, husbands are told to make every effort to *ginosko* their wives and thus to learn—or understand—them and to live with them according to that knowledge.

The husband who has learned his wife knows she wants a hardworking husband. He applies that knowledge and lives with her in an understanding way by providing for her week in and week out.

Husbands Value Their Wives by Working Hard

Peter says to "[give] honor to the wife," and the word for "honor" is *time*. It means "a valuing by which the price is fixed."[xxvi] Eight times in Scripture, *time* is translated as "price" because it refers to the value of something. Here are two examples of its use:

- "The chief priests took the silver pieces and said, 'It is not lawful to put them into the treasury, because they are the price (*time*) of blood'" (Matthew 27:6).
- "Peter said, 'Ananias, why has Satan filled your heart to lie to the Holy Spirit and keep back part of the price (*time*) of the land for yourself?'" (Acts 5:3).

Peter's message to husbands is clear: Recognize the value of your wife and honor her as a result.

The phrase "to the wife" has an interesting application as well. The Greek word for "wife" is *gyne*, occurring 220 times in the New Testament.[xxvii] The word is used twice in 1 Peter 3, in verses 1 and 5: "Wives (*gyne*), likewise, be submissive…In former times, the holy women (*gyne*)." But the phrase "to the wife" is only one word in Greek, *gynaikeios*, and this is the only place it occurs in Scripture.[xxviii] While *gyne* is a noun, *gynaikeios* is an adjective meaning "of or belonging to a woman, feminine, female."

Peter is not commanding husbands to honor their wives simply for the sake of honoring them. Instead, husbands are commanded to find value in their wives' femininity and praise them for it. Ladies, young or old, single or married, should celebrate their femininity and enjoy the beauty God has given them.

If we think something is valuable, we'll work hard for it. The student who thinks a degree is valuable will work hard in school. The employee who thinks a promotion is valuable will work hard to be promoted. The consumer who thinks a product is valuable will work hard for the money to make the purchase. Similarly, the husband who thinks his wife is valuable will work hard to care for her. His efforts will help her feel loved. Conversely, the lazy husband communicates through his actions that he doesn't think his wife is valuable enough to work hard for her. His lack of effort will cause his wife to feel unloved.

Husbands Use Their Strength to Work Hard

We don't see transgender females wanting to compete in male sports, but there are growing examples of transgender men competing in female sports. Gavin Hubbard set New Zealand junior weightlifting records in 1998.[xxix] In 2012, he became a transgender, changed his name to Laurel, and competed in the 2017 Australian

International and Australian Open weightlifting competition where he won the gold medal.[xxx] The transgender men, who have no business competing in women's sports, typically win because God created the genders with physical differences.

Peter says wives are "the weaker vessel," but this does not mean morally, intellectually, or spiritually. Some women are stronger than their husbands in these areas. This is speaking of men being stronger physically. The Amplified Bible says, "honoring the woman as [physically] the weaker vessel." Women are approximately 40–50 percent weaker than men in the upper body and 30–40 percent weaker in the lower body.[xxxi] It is also important to notice that it says "weaker" instead of "weak." Men are physically weak, too. We get sick. We can be injured. We are susceptible to age and eventually die. Our physical weakness should be a reminder to us to be sensitive to our wife's physical weakness.

Why did God make men physically stronger? One reason is so men can protect women! One of the evilest tragedies is when men use their strength to hurt women. God gave men greater strength so they could be protective; therefore, when men physically abuse women, they're doubly sinning:

- They're committing a sin of commission through their behavior.
- They're committing a sin of omission by failing to use their strength for the reason God gave it to them.

Treating our wives as the weaker vessel means making our wives feel safe and protected. Colossians 3:19 instructs: "Husbands, love your wives and *do not be harsh with them*" (NIV, ESV). Wives should not have to fear verbal, emotional, or physical abuse. Rather, every wife should be confident that her husband will step up and deal with conflict or danger. Every husband, as best as he can, should put himself between his wife and anything that might threaten her physically, mentally, emotionally, or spiritually.

God also gave men greater strength so we can work hard. As already discussed in Chapter One, God told Adam, "In toil you shall eat of [the ground]...In the sweat of your face you shall eat bread" (Genesis 3:17–19). God said work would be hard for us, but He graciously gave us the strength needed. The man who isn't working hard isn't using his strength for one of the premier reasons it was given to him.

Even though women are physically "weaker," with the words "heirs together of the grace of life," Peter prevents his readers from thinking wives are at all inferior to their husbands, because the word "heirs" speaks of equality. Only males were heirs in the Roman world. The gospel makes women fellow heirs and co-inheritors, which was a radical concept in the ancient world. This reminds husbands that even though they have more authority, their wives are still identical to them in terms of spiritual privilege and importance. Husbands who see their wives this way will work hard because they want to care and provide for daughters of the King.

Keeping His Prayers from Being "Chopped Down"

If the world isn't trying to feminize men by convincing them that transgenderism is acceptable, then it's trying to push them to the other extreme of chauvinism and hyper-masculinity that values physical strength above all else. God wants husbands to resist both extremes and be strong spiritual leaders; therefore, 1 Peter 3:7 ends with a sobering warning that should cause any Christian husband to treat his wife well: "that your prayers may not be hindered." Scripture teaches that sin hinders our prayers:

- "When you spread out your hands, I will hide My eyes from you; even though you make many prayers, I will not hear. Your hands are full of blood" (Isaiah 1:15).
- "If I regard iniquity in my heart, the Lord will not hear" (Psalm 66:18).
- "God does not hear sinners; but if anyone is a worshiper of God and does His will, He hears him" (John 9:31).

Peter specifies one sin that prevents God from hearing the prayers of husbands—the sin of mistreating their wives. The Greek word for "hindered" is *ekkopto*, which means "cut off; of a tree."[xxxii] The Amplified Bible says: "in order that your prayers may not be hindered and cut off." Jesus twice used the word regarding cutting down a fruit tree:

- "Every tree that does not bear good fruit is cut down (*ekkopto*)" (Matthew 7:19).
- "Look, for three years I have come seeking fruit on this fig tree and find none. Cut it down (*ekkopto*)" (Luke 13:7).

Why would God use the same word for cutting down a fruit tree to describe a husband's prayers being hindered? The intended image is of a husband's prayers being fruitless or "chopped down." A necessity for every husband to be a good spiritual leader is having God hear his prayers, and it is so important to God that husbands treat their wives well that He says He will not hear them if they disobey in this area. The only prayer God will hear from husbands when they mistreat their wives is a prayer of repentance: "I am very sorry for the way I treated my wife."

I am ashamed to say there have been times I have left for the office only to have to turn around and head home to make things right with Katie. I knew I had not treated her the way I should, and when I arrived at my office to pray, God would not hear me.

The nineteenth-century preacher Charles Spurgeon said, "To true believers prayer is so invaluable that the danger of hindering it is used by Peter as a motive…in their marriage relationships."[xxxiii] Sadly, some men have such a low regard for prayer that this warning does not cause them to treat their wives any differently. One reason this attitude is so terrible is that the passage is largely about wives submitting to their husbands; wives will have a much easier time submitting to spiritual men who are fearful of having their prayers hindered. A wife who has a husband who values having his prayers heard by God more than almost anything else, will have a much easier time submitting to him, as the previous verses described.

One of the most straightforward ways husbands prevent their prayers from being "chopped down" is through hard work, because this allows them to care for their wives. If a husband takes his spiritual leadership seriously, he will work hard to ensure God hears his prayers. Conversely, the lazy husband reveals he doesn't take his spiritual leadership seriously, because he's comfortable having his prayers chopped down.

Lazy Men Are Worse Than Unbelievers

First Timothy 5:8 provides husbands the encouragement they need to avoid giving in to the temptation to be lazy: "But if anyone does not provide for his own, and especially for those of his household, he has denied the faith and is worse than an unbeliever." The pronouns "his" and "he" show Paul has men in view, because God expects husbands to provide financially for their families.

A criticism couldn't be stronger than saying that someone is "worse than an unbeliever." How can Paul say this since we tend to think nothing is worse than being an unbeliever? He says this because many unbelievers do care for their loved ones. When a man fails to provide for his wife and children, he's committing a sin even many non-Christians don't commit.

God's Disdain for Lazy Men

Eglon was the king of the Moabites. He was evil, which makes his example more sobering: if God shows such contempt toward a lazy, unbelieving man, how does He feel toward lazy, believing men? Eglon's story takes place in the book of Judges. For context, Judges contains cycles following the same steps:

1. Israel turns from God
2. God turns Israel over to another nation to be disciplined
3. Israel cries out to God for deliverance
4. God raises up a judge to deliver them
5. The judge delivers Israel and the cycle repeats

Israel rebelled against God, and He turned them over to Eglon, king of the Moabites. Israel cried out to God, and God raised up Ehud, a judge, to deliver them. Eglon oppressed the Israelites and made them give him money. Ehud was tasked with taking the money to Eglon, probably because he led Israel at the time. Scripture presents Eglon as an obese, lazy, selfish man:

- "Eglon was a very fat man" (Judges 3:17).
- "[Eglon] was sitting upstairs in his cool private chamber" (Judges 3:20).
- "Eglon's servants [found]…the doors of the upper room locked. So they said, "He is probably attending to his needs in the cool chamber" (Judges 3:24).

Eglon showed little concern for others. There is no indication he worked, served, or did anything of substance. He selfishly kept himself locked in his comfortable room. Nobody had access to him except special visitors and servants he kept on hand to attend to his needs. Ehud only reached him because he brought him money. Judges 3:20–22 records:

Ehud said, "I have a message from God for you." So he arose from his seat. Then Ehud reached with his left hand, took the dagger from his right thigh, and thrust it into his belly. Even the hilt went in after the blade, and the fat closed over the blade, for he did not draw the dagger out of his belly; and his entrails came out.

Perhaps nobody reveals God's disdain for lazy men better than Eglon. Ehud's words reveal God had him assassinate the Moabite king for his oppressive, selfish lifestyle.

While most men aren't going to stoop to the level of Eglon's laziness and selfishness, we can engage in these sins to lesser degrees. Two reminders should keep us men on guard. First, in God's eyes, the man who fails to care for his family is worse than an unbeliever (1 Timothy 5:8). Second, one of the best ways for a husband to "dwell with [his wife] with understanding" is to work hard to provide for her and their children. The man who keeps these reminders before him will surely be working God's way. Thus, he will be well suited by his example to encourage his wife and children in doing their work God's way, as we shall discover in the following chapters.

Chapter Ten

Women Should Work, but How and Where?

The discussion of men working is straightforward, but it is not so for women. Let me capture the predicament by inviting you to picture the following: a pastor comfortably and boldly preaches that men should have a job and work. Can you picture a pastor preaching about women getting a job and working with the same comfort and boldness? Why not?

The pastor rightly is a man and some in our gender-confused world object on those grounds.[1] There is a clash in our culture with

---

[1] Church leaders are identified as men. Consider the qualifications in 1 Timothy 3:1–5: "If a man desires the position of a bishop, he desires a good work...the husband of one wife...one who rules his own house well, having his children in submission." We see the same when Paul discusses elders in Titus 1:6, 9: "If a man is blameless, the husband of one wife...holding fast the faithful word as he has been taught." When churches have female pastors or elders, they have rejected the teaching of God's Word. In 1 Timothy 2:12–14, the apostle Paul instructs: "I do not permit a woman to teach or to have authority over a man, but to be in silence. For Adam was formed first, then Eve. And Adam was not deceived, but the woman being deceived, fell into transgression." While it sounds as though Adam is commended for not being deceived and Eve is condemned for being deceived, it is actually the opposite. Eve was not as much

resurgent feminism creeping into the church, but we must hold to the clear teaching of the Bible. We have trouble saying whether women should work outside the home, but we can resolve this issue by taking an honest look at God's Word.

Just as the curse was pronounced on Adam's work, it also was pronounced on Eve's labors. God's words reveal the two areas in which He primarily wants women invested. In Genesis 3:16, He said to Eve, "I will greatly multiply your sorrow and your conception; in pain you shall bring forth children; your desire shall be for your husband, and he shall rule over you."

God mentioned a woman's children and husband because this is where most of her time and energy are committed. When women are addressed throughout Scripture, their husbands, children, and homes are emphasized. For example, 1 Timothy 2:15 says women "will be saved in childbearing if they continue in faith, love, and holiness, with self-control." We know from the rest of Scripture that this doesn't mean women are saved by having children, but what does it mean?

First, raising children is the primary sphere of ministry in which women serve the Lord and work out their salvation. Second, in this verse, "saved" is being used synonymously with sanctified. Any mother can tell you raising children is sanctifying! Does anything teach patience, gentleness, self-denial, and self-sacrifice more than mothering? My wife, Katie, says nothing in her life causes her to

---

at fault because she was deceived while Adam was more at fault because he sinned knowingly.

Sometimes people ask: "Why can't women be in leadership over men in the church or in the home?" It has nothing to do with talent or gifting. Some women are fantastic teachers and leaders, and they should use their skills over other women and children. What it does have to do with is Adam being created first and Eve's being deceived. Beyond that, we cannot say because those are the only two reasons Paul gives in 1 Timothy 2:13–14. The real question is not "Why can't women?" The real question—and it is the same question we often face—is: "Will we submit to God's Word?"

cling to the Lord and trust Him more than having children. This is one of the reasons children are a blessing (Psalm 127:3).

Several verses in Scripture encourage women to focus on their homes, husbands, and children:

- "The wise woman *builds her house*" (Proverbs 14:1).
- "I desire that the younger widows marry, bear children, *manage the house*" (1 Timothy 5:14).
- "Older women…admonish the young women to love their husbands, to love their children, to be discreet, chaste, *homemakers*" (Titus 2:3–5).

In Chapter Eight we discussed small things that are despised in our eyes. The lives of women working at home might seem to be filled with small, despised things such as laundry, meals, and cleaning. My heart especially goes out to young ladies who are made to feel like they're doing a small thing when they help their mother with the house or other children. If God wants women—young or old—to do these things, then they aren't small to Him, which means they shouldn't be considered small to us.

Women will be tempted to pursue something different for themselves, but they're doing a great thing in God's eyes when they care for their homes and families, and lead quiet lives. J.R. Miller said, "The woman who makes a sweet, beautiful home, filling it with love and prayer and purity, is doing something better than anything else her hands could find to do beneath the skies."[xxxiv]

The Virtuous Wife

The lengthiest passage for wives is Proverbs 31:13–16. One might say that it is a description of the ideal woman. Interestingly, these verses were written when women were not only legal possessions of men, but their sphere of influence traditionally did not extend beyond the home and raising children. So, what this passage includes as attributes of the "perfect woman" stands out in even starker contrast to what one might consider a stereotype of the biblical wife. Proverbs 31:13–16 deal specifically with the Virtuous Wife's job description:

> She seeks wool and flax, and willingly works with her hands. She is like the merchant ships, she brings her food from afar. She also rises while it is yet night, and provides food for her household, and a portion for her maidservants. She considers a field and buys it; from her profits she plants a vineyard.

She gathers materials to take care of her family. She is diligent with her hands and journeys to secure the best food for her loved ones. Her hardworking nature is shown in the way she gets up before dawn to have food prepared, not just for her family, but also for the servants. She is industrious and resourceful as she buys a field and then reinvests the profits to make more money. This is important because it shows that women can engage in work that provides for their families financially. Simply put—men are not the only ones who can make money.

The passage then elaborates on the ways she further cares for her family, the poor, and herself. Proverbs 31:17–22 states:

> She girds herself with strength, and strengthens her arms. She perceives that her merchandise is good, and her lamp does not go out by night...She extends her hand to the poor. Yes, she reaches out her hands to the needy. She is not afraid of snow for her household, for all her household is clothed with scarlet. She makes tapestry for herself; her clothing is fine linen and purple.

Her hardworking nature allowed her to be strong and healthy. Everything she made for her family, such as food and clothing, was of high quality, and she was willing to work late into the night to produce it. Her inventory was large enough to help those in poverty. She anticipated her family's needs and made sure they were met. While providing for others, she did not neglect to provide high-quality possessions for herself.

Verse 24 says, "She makes linen garments and sells them, and supplies sashes for the merchants." Her efforts bless many. While this took place, she was careful to keep her home a priority: "She watches over the ways of her household, and does not eat the bread of idleness" (Proverbs 31:27).

The Virtuous Wife is a skilled homemaker, but there are also verses about her industriousness as she works outside the home. In the New Testament, there are two examples of godly women working:

- Lydia "was a seller of purple...who worshiped God" (Acts 16:14).
- Priscilla and her husband Aquila, "were tentmakers" (Acts 18:3).

How do we reconcile these two investments of time and energy for women—working and homemaking—that seem to be at odds with each other? The simple answer is women worked without neglecting the care of their families. They probably performed many of these activities from their homes.

Whatever work a wife does should still allow her to care for her husband, children, and the home itself. These are her most important ministries; therefore, they should never suffer from anything she engages in.

Threats to Women's Priorities: Pursuit of Wealth

The wealth a wife accumulates caring for herself and her family is not the threat to her priorities. Instead, the threat is the pursuit of wealth that comes from keeping up with neighbors, or pursuing a fancier, more glamorous lifestyle. While it's reasonable for women to work for the reasons previously mentioned, it's unreasonable for them to work for selfish pursuits that cause them to neglect their priorities. No godly woman will look back and say:

- "I'm so glad we got this bigger house, even though it meant hardly seeing my children."
- "This extra income has been such a blessing, even though it meant late nights away from my husband."
- "I'm so thankful for that promotion, even though it meant rarely being home."

Threats to Women's Priorities: Self-Worth

Some women don't find the same satisfaction caring for their homes, husbands, and children that they find in the workplace. Money, promotions, praise, and the opportunity to compete with men can appeal to their pride.

Romans 12:2 says, "Do not be conformed to this world, but be transformed by the renewing of your mind, that you may prove what is that good and acceptable and perfect will of God." Women have been conformed to this world when they work outside the home because they:

- Believe focusing on home and family gives them less value
- Want to find self-worth they're unable to find caring for their home and family
- Don't experience the fulfillment they crave caring for their home and family

When any of these situations occur, women have been influenced by the world versus Scripture. They must renew their minds by reading the Bible.

Since fulfilling God's priorities for women gives them their greatest value, when they focus on these priorities, they should experience their greatest sense of self-worth. The woman fulfilling the role and responsibilities God has given her should feel more valuable than being a company's CEO.

Threats to Women's Priorities: Laziness

Even when women are home, they can still neglect their husband, children, or home. They must be intentional to ensure they aren't overly invested in frivolous activities. There are plenty of ways women can waste their time. For some women, maybe their priorities are talking on the phone, watching television, using the internet, or surfing Facebook.

Scripture doesn't forbid engaging in these activities, but it does forbid women from neglecting the priorities God has given them. The Proverbs 31 woman engaged in several activities—many could be called hobbies—but they benefited her husband, children, and home.

Women Have Become Unhappier Working Outside the Home

Although our culture presents women climbing the corporate ladder positively, research suggests otherwise. Females working outside the home are finding less satisfaction in their jobs and many long to return to their families.

Researcher Daniele Lup, a senior lecturer in quantitative sociology at Middlesex University, studied ten years of data from thousands of male and female employees who were promoted to upper and lower management roles. She concluded that men reported an increase in job satisfaction after being promoted, but women experienced significantly less satisfaction when promoted.[xxxv] Even when women were advancing in corporate America, their joy was plummeting.

In 2009, the IZA Institute of Labor Economics published, "The Paradox of Declining Female Happiness."[xxxvi] The study found that in the 1970s, women rated their overall life satisfaction higher than men. Since then, with more women working outside the home than ever before, their scores continually decreased while men's scores stayed around the same. By the 1990s, women were unhappier than men even though their salaries went from earning less than 60 percent of a man's median salary to earning over 75 percent of it. In other words, even while women continued to seek satisfaction in the business world, and experience greater success, their happiness headed the other direction.

Important Considerations

Life does not always go the way we expect. Some women don't have husbands because either they're widowed or they never married. Their greatest desire might be staying home, but they must work to provide for themselves. A young wife might long to care for children, but perhaps she's been unable to have a child. I have known couples who would like the wife to be able to stay home, but an injured husband or a financial emergency, required the wife to work outside the home.

For women experiencing these (and there are other) situations, they should never be made to feel condemned because, in such situations, the best way for them to care for their families (or themselves) is by working outside the home.

Women who keep the above truths in mind will surely be working God's way. And what of her children? How do they work God's way? Let's read on to find out!

Chapter Eleven

Youths Should Set an Example

Rarely do people with lazy childhoods grow up to be diligent adults, because they'll bring the habits they developed in their childhood into adulthood; therefore, the best approach is to start training children to have a strong work ethic when they're young. The work they do depends on their strength and maturity, but even at a young age, they can do jobs around the house, and sometimes even in the surrounding neighborhood.

In the church I pastor, we strive to take care of our needs ourselves as opposed to paying people to do it for us. This means we have a schedule for families to clean the church, instead of hiring a janitor to do it. We have church workdays versus hiring people for maintenance and repairs. When church cleaning and workdays take place, families perform these tasks together. Children work alongside adults. Unfortunately, in some churches, children might be the least likely to serve, but this is the opposite of what should be the case.

In Ephesians 6:1 and Colossians 3:20, Paul charged, "Children, obey your parents in the Lord, for this is right," and "Children, obey your parents in all things, for this is well pleasing to the Lord." Performing chores faithfully and with a good attitude is one of the primary ways children obey their parents. Parents can remind their children that 2 Thessalonians 3:10 teaches that people who don't work shouldn't eat. Are parents going to starve their children? No, but rare is the child who wouldn't benefit from the lesson that missing a meal teaches. How many children would work more diligently if they were told the meal wouldn't be served until all the work is done?

Unfortunately, society makes children think they aren't adults until they're twenty-one, but they can behave maturely years earlier. Paul said, "When I was a child, I spoke as a child, I understood as a child, I thought as a child; but when I became a man, I put away childish things" (1 Corinthians 13:11). According to this verse, becoming an adult has more to do with putting away childish things than it has to do with age. Some children are mature because of the childish things they've put away. Conversely, some older people are immature, because of the childish things they haven't put away.

According to a 2017 study published in *The New England Journal of Medicine*, 57 percent of today's children will be obese by the time they're thirty-five.[xxxvii] The Centers for Disease Control found that obesity puts children at risk for many chronic health problems, such as diabetes, heart disease, asthma, joint pain, and sleep disorders.[xxxviii]

In 2017, Harvard Health Medical School recommended children be active for at least one hour per day because, along with genetics and diet, the other major factor contributing to health problems is physical inactivity. Long periods of time in front of screens are the most common culprit.[xxxix] A 1995 study in the *American Journal of Clinical Nutrition* found that children are 21.5 percent more likely to be overweight if they watch four hours of television per day.[xl]

This bar of one hour of activity per day is so low I'm surprised it must be set. While the activity could be walking, playing outside, or riding a bike, chores and work have the added benefits of teaching responsibility and building character.

When children grow up without learning to work, they become entitled teenagers and young adults. They expect everything to be done for them and given to them. The premier example is youth suing their parents.

In 2014, ABC News reported that Rachel Canning sued her parents to force them to pay for her private college tuition. Her father shared that "she didn't want to follow our house rules concerning curfew and chores" and felt entitled to "Private school, new car, [and] college education."[xli]

In 2016, the CBC reported that Darren Randall sued his parents for posting baby pictures of him on social media. Darren said, "I had no say in my image being on the internet." When asked why he requested $350,000, he answered, "It's a small price to pay for a decade of humiliation."[xlii]

In 2019, World News Daily reported that Anthony Dwight sued his parents for being born white. His lawyer argued, "My client did not choose to live this kind of life. Why would he have to carry the burden of hundreds of years of slavery and racism all because his parents had the selfish desire to bring another white child into this world."[xliii]

Ephesians 6:2 commands children to honor their parents, and these individuals have done the opposite.

The LaPierre Household

In our household, we allow our kids to be bored instead of striving to entertain them. We haven't introduced video games to them, and we limit what and how much they watch because we want to prevent them from developing certain appetites. This causes our children to find things to do, but we only make available what we believe is beneficial for them. We choose activities that foster creativity, such as music, art, reading, writing, and building. We purchase books, musical instruments, art supplies, and toys such as Legos, Duplos, and K'Nex. We typically avoid toys that require batteries or electricity. Since we want our kids playing outside, we invest in bikes, skates, scooters, jump ropes, and sidewalk chalk.

While we're not always able to allow our kids to do what they enjoy—sometimes they must do chores they dislike—we try to see what interests them and help them grow in these areas as early as possible. I've told my kids that since Katie and I think it's important for them to work, we'll try to support their business efforts as long as they honor the Lord.

Our oldest child, Rhea, is twelve years old. She enjoys art and organizing. Last year she started selling personalized cards and signs with Bible verses. A few months ago, she started selling clothes and other items on eBay. We turned a corner of our basement into her craft room, where she does her work and keeps her supplies.

Our second oldest child, Ricky, is eleven. He enjoys outdoor work, such as landscaping. We encouraged him to walk around the neighborhood and ask people if he could mow their lawns. He ended up with so many jobs we had to tell him he couldn't accept anymore because he wouldn't have time to do his schoolwork and chores. We're moving everything from the shed behind the house into the garage, so the shed can become his utility room with his tools, lawnmower, and weed eater.

Our third child, Johnny, is nine, and he loves animals. He asked neighbors if he could walk their dogs. Recently, he expressed interest in breeding and selling dogs, so we built him a kennel. When he gets older, he'll probably be Ricky's first employee for his landscaping business.

I've been reading the manuscript for *Work and Rest God's Way* with my kids, and I told them I'd give them a dollar for every grammar mistake they find. We all benefit. My kids are reading a Christian book and improving their grammar, and I'm getting a book (hopefully) without spelling errors.

Addressing One of My Weaknesses as a Father

The summer after eighth grade I flew from California to upstate New York to work on my uncle's dairy farm. This was when I realized I wanted to work in a nice, air-conditioned building, versus outside. As my sons have gotten older, it's become apparent that they're the opposite of me: they want to work outside.

Growing up I focused on athletics and academics. I went to school, practiced for a sport, came home, did homework, went to bed, and did the same thing the next day. This prepared me for college, but the downside is that I lack the automotive, mechanical, and hands-on skills many fathers have to pass along to their children.

Even if you're more prepared to teach your children than I was, no parents can teach their children everything. For those areas of inexperience, we have a few choices.

First, we can learn alongside our children. This allows us to acquire a new skill and, even more importantly, spend quality time with them.

Second, we can find knowledgeable people for our children to learn from. Recently, one of our church deacons built shelves in our garage. My sons were with him to learn woodworking. I asked one of the men in our church to let me know the next time he was going to the range with his sons. I brought my boys, and they learned how to shoot guns.

The third possibility is self-directed learning. We can purchase books for our kids to read and have them watch instructional videos on the internet. Rhea regularly watches art videos. Since Ricky was given the shed for his tools, he's been watching videos about organizing a workbench. Johnny's been watching videos about dog breeding.

The Journey to a Family Business

Growing up, I wanted to go to college, graduate, and then become a teacher and coach. The idea of having my own business wasn't attractive or unattractive because it simply wasn't on my radar. When I began pastoring at Woodland Christian Church, I noticed men had their own businesses that involved their children, such as a dairy farm and machine shop. Another father built his house with his kids. Since I lacked these men's skills, I had to figure out what I could do that would involve my children.

As an author and speaker, my children package and mail my books, and sell them at my engagements. They set up my booth and run it before, during, and after conferences. I stop by to check in, but they handle things well enough that I'm able to spend my time ministering to attendees.

My kids used to have their products at my booth, but now they have their own booths to sell their flowers, artworks, signs, and offer face painting. This allows them to make money, develop communication skills, and build relationships.

With my experience as an author, I can help them publish their own books in the future. Recently, I started working with my oldest children on their own websites.

They learn songs to sing at conferences and our church. While they haven't always enjoyed this, we challenge them that it's a way to serve God and others. They've been taking music lessons for years, and recently they started using instruments, such as the piano and ukulele, in their performances. As the kids got older, more instruments will be introduced, and perhaps there will be a LaPierre Family Band.

Don't Let Your Youth Hinder You

Accounts in Scripture demonstrate that God uses youths. Unfortunately, when we think of the twelve disciples, we probably think they were in their thirties or forties. According to Luke 3:23, "Jesus Himself began His ministry at about thirty years of age." Disciples were generally younger than their teacher; therefore, it's likely the disciples were in their twenties. In Matthew 11:25, Luke 10:21, and John 13:33, Jesus referred to them as "little children" and "babes," probably indicating they were several years younger than Him. The article, "How Old Were Christ's Disciples?" in the journal, *The Biblical World*, states they were, "not far from sixteen or seventeen."[xliv] John, who wrote the Book of Revelation in his nineties, was probably a teenager when he became Jesus' disciple.

There's at least one account that indicates all of them were under twenty, except Peter, which explains why he was the leader of the group and the only one married (Matthew 8:14). Matthew 17:24–27 records Jesus and Peter paid the temple tax, which according to Exodus 30:13–14, was required of everyone twenty years and older. All the disciples were present, but Jesus only provided money for Peter and Himself, because the other eleven weren't old enough to have to pay it yet.

A few of the disciples had established jobs. Peter, Andrew, James, and John were fishermen. This might make them look older, but Jewish schooling ended around twelve years old, which gave them time to begin work at young ages.

Why might Jesus have wanted the disciples to be young? They had so much ahead of them, such as laying the "foundation of the church" (Ephesians 2:20). They were just getting started when Jesus' earthly ministry ended.

When the prophet Jeremiah was young, he wrote:

> Then the word of the LORD came to me, saying:
> "Before I formed you in the womb I knew you; before
> you were born I sanctified you; I ordained you a
> prophet to the nations."
> Then said I: "Ah, Lord God! Behold, I cannot speak,
> for I am a youth."

117

But the LORD said to me: "Do not say, 'I am a youth,' for you shall go to all to whom I send you, and whatever I command you, you shall speak. Do not be afraid of their faces, for I am with you to deliver you," says the LORD (Jeremiah 1:4–8).

Jeremiah thought he was too young to serve God and speak for Him, so he responded poorly when God asked him to be a prophet. God did not reply to his objection by saying something like, "Oh, sorry, I didn't realize you were so young. Don't worry about serving Me yet. Spend the next decade goofing off, playing video games, watching movies, and then you can become a prophet when you're older." Instead, God expected Jeremiah to preach to nations as a youth.

Even though young people today aren't called to be prophets or one of the twelve apostles, they should still see themselves as Jesus' disciples. He gives them gifts to minister to the body of Christ. They shouldn't believe the notion that they're too young to serve God or others. He has special purposes for them to fulfill.

Being an Example in Five Ways

Sometimes when people are in their teens or twenties, they don't see themselves as examples. They think nobody looks up to them until they're older, perhaps in their thirties, forties, or even fifties. Older Christians worsen the perception when they make youths feel like they don't have anything to offer.

Scripture commands the opposite of this: "Let no one despise your youth, but be an example to the believers in word, in conduct, in love, in faith, in purity" (1 Timothy 4:12). Since no age is specified, it seems youths should be an example to people of any age in five ways.

First, in Word

The way youths speak should set an example. When Jesus was twelve years old, His parents found Him "in the temple, sitting in the midst of the teachers, both listening to them and asking them questions. And all who heard Him were astonished at His understanding and answers" (Luke 2:46–47).

Yes, Jesus was God in the flesh, but youths can still learn from His example. First, they can listen well and ask good questions. Second, they can speak well by demonstrating understanding and sharing wisdom.

Second, in Conduct

The way youths behave and carry themselves should set an example, and I'll use my children to illustrate why this is so important. My greatest desire for them is to see them love and serve Christ. First Corinthians 11:1 says, "Be imitators of me, as I am of Christ." Having good examples is so important Paul told his readers to imitate him.[1]

The examples I follow in my life are typically men in the church who are about ten years older than I am, or another way to say it is they're experiencing the next season of life. Do you think my children look up to the same people that I do? No. They look up to the people a few years older than them, or in their next season of life. Since my oldest of eight is twelve, all my children are looking up to youths!

I've told the young men in my church who, through their conduct, are setting good examples for my boys, and the other boys in the church, how much I appreciate them. They treat the young ladies around them with respect, and they serve and act with

---

[1] See also 1 Corinthians 4:16, Philippians 3:17, 4:9, 1 Thessalonians 1:6, and 2 Thessalonians 3:7, 9.

maturity for their age. They also set good examples in working hard: they have jobs, and they look for ways to serve the church.

I've told the young ladies in the church who, through their conduct, are setting good examples for my girls, and the other girls in the church, how much I appreciate them. They carry themselves with respect, dress modestly, embrace biblical femininity, and reject the world's feminism. Youths should see themselves as important examples in conduct, especially to those younger than them.

Third, in Love

The way youths treat others should set an example. The world thinks love is a feeling or emotion, but Scripture says it is actions. First Corinthians 13, "The Love Chapter," is filled with verbs (action words), versus adjectives (describing words). We show love by what we do for others.

Paul said, "The unmarried man and woman are *anxious about the things of the Lord, how to please the Lord*" (1 Corinthians 7:32, 34). The verses describe single adults, but because youths are typically single, they have application for them too. Without the responsibilities married people have, such as caring for a spouse and possibly children, youths have more time and energy to love others. They can serve in the church, help families, engage in evangelism, and visit the elderly.

Fourth, in Faith

Youths should have a zeal for God that sets an example for others. Few things can encourage senior saints more than seeing young people with passionate hearts for the Lord.

Fifth, in Purity

Let me back up and get a little momentum into this fifth word, by asking you to consider why Paul said youths should set an example? Isn't this a little counterintuitive? Don't we expect older people to set an example? Let me answer this by sharing two things that happen as I get older.

First, I gain credibility because as I age, people think I have more wisdom and knowledge. This is biblical: "Wisdom is with the aged, and understanding [with] length of days" (Job 12:12).

Second, I lose credibility, at least when I talk about certain things, because the older I am, the more conservative people expect me to become. When people speak conservatively in their sixties, seventies, or eighties, listeners think, "Well, of course, you're going to say that, because you're old!" This is part of why, as long as I'm still young (at least to some people), I try to preach as boldly as I can on conservative topics.

Paul said, "God did not call us to be *impure*, but to live a *holy* life" (1 Thessalonians 4:7 NIV). Impurity and holiness are opposites, so purity and holiness are synonyms.

This brings us to the reason youths should set an example "in purity" and holiness. They have the most credibility! It's one thing when older people are pure and holy, but few things are as powerful as youths leading pure and holy lives.

Grace and Work

Let me be perfectly clear as we come to the end of this chapter. Children must be rooted in the enabling grace of God to work—or do anything for that matter—that pleases Him. Do not come away from this chapter, thinking that if you simply organize your family a certain way, that all will go well with your children. Believe the high and foundational truth that the gospel working in your children's hearts is the work they need more than anything else.

With that said, second only to pointing your children to Jesus, teaching them to work is necessary to be faithful Christian parents. This will help prevent your children from developing entitlement mentalities, prepare them for marriage and families, and give them the tools they need to serve the Lord and others as they get older.

As I wrote in the Introduction, my dad made us work hard when we were growing up. I didn't appreciate it at the time. I used to wish I had a "normal" father who would let us spend weekends and summers playing. Now I couldn't be more thankful. Most children and youth don't appreciate having to work hard when they're young, but few things will make them more thankful toward their parents when they become adults.

What about working *too much*, whether men, women, or children? Is that possible? Can a good (moral) thing, such as work, become a bad thing? If so, how do we know when we are no longer working God's way, but instead have developed a sinful relationship toward work? In the next chapter, we'll explore the answers to these questions.

Chapter Twelve

The Danger of Workaholism

Picture a young father, Brian, whose parents made him work hard when he was growing up. Although he didn't like it at the time, now that he has a family of his own, he appreciates the way they raised him. To provide for his family, he's been putting in more hours than ever before. Over time he begins to value his work hours more than his family time. Church attendance has become infrequent because he's convinced his paycheck can care for him better than God. Most of his thoughts are consumed with accumulating wealth and securing a reputation for himself.

He's anxious, exhausted, and his health is suffering, but he can't stop checking emails, returning phone calls, and sending text messages. Every communication, project, deal, sale, and offer is important. He stays awake at night worried about the next review, promotion, or deadline.

Productivity is so important he's critical of others who make mistakes or don't achieve as much as him. What his boss thinks is more important than what his wife, children, or God think. He pursues his job with the same passion with which he used to pursue Christ.

Brian's job became an idol. He turned a good thing into a god thing. Like Brian, we have the potential to ruin even the blessings God gives us because of our sinfulness. One such example took place with the bronze serpent. Israel complained, and as a judgment, God sent poisonous serpents into the camp:

> Therefore the people came to Moses, and said, "We have sinned, for we have spoken against the LORD and against you; pray to the LORD that He take away the serpents from us." So Moses prayed for the people.
> Then the LORD said to Moses, "Make a fiery serpent, and set it on a pole; and it shall be that everyone who is bitten, when he looks at it, shall live." So Moses made a bronze serpent, and put it on a pole; and so it was, if a serpent had bitten anyone, when he looked at the bronze serpent, he lived" (Numbers 21:7–9).

Tragically, over time, people began to worship the bronze serpent. When Hezekiah reformed the nation and destroyed the idolatry, he had to include the bronze serpent, which by then had developed its own name:

> [Hezekiah] removed the high places and broke the sacred pillars, cut down the wooden image and broke in pieces the bronze serpent that Moses had made; for until those days the children of Israel burned incense to it, *and called it Nehushtan*" (2 Kings 18:4).

The object that brought miraculous healing became an idol. Nehushtan is a reminder that we must be on guard against taking any of God's blessings—such as marriage, children, homes, relationships, money, or jobs—and letting our relationships to them become sinful. Scripture doesn't forbid any of the above, but we are forbidden from making them idols. Brian's job, and our jobs, are no more sinful than the bronze serpent; however, when we worship them, they become Nehushtan.

When Our Relationship to Work Becomes Sinful

> Their land is also full of idols; *they worship the work of
> their own hands*, that which their own fingers have made
> (Isaiah 2:8).

The people in Isaiah's day worshiped their work, and we can
worship our work too. Just as we can rest too much (laziness), we
can work too much (workaholism). As we discussed in Chapter
One, work is moral. When we commit the sin of workaholism, work
didn't suddenly become immoral and sinful. Instead, our
relationship to work became sinful.

Workaholics have the same relationship to their work that
addicts have to alcohol, drugs, or pornography. Everything else in
their lives—family, friends, church, health, and rest—takes a
backseat to their jobs. Time and energy committed to anyone and
anything else is always rushed or neglected.

In the past, people couldn't begin working before the sun came
up, and they stopped working when the sun went down. Now
electricity allows us to have our lights, computers, and cell phones
on around the clock. Our twenty-four-hour days seem restrictive
because it's harder to fit in everything we think we need to do. Since
society promotes "bigger and better," we feel the pressure to keep
up, and we find ourselves busier than ever. Covetousness has never
been a stronger temptation. The only solution seems to be more
work. We can become like machines moving from one task to the
next. We end up overworked, under-rested, and spiritually
undernourished.

It's not wise, kind, humble, or impressive when we take on more
than we can handle. It shows a lack of wisdom because of the
problems it causes. We know our relationship to work has become
sinful when it drowns out the areas of our lives the Lord wants us

investing in, such as our spouse, parents, children, friends, and church.

Answer these questions honestly to help determine whether you struggle with workaholism:

- When you're supposed to be resting, does your mind return to work?
- Are you able to detach from your job, or do you bring your work home with you?
- Do you obsess about your job when you're not working, thereby removing the distinction between work and rest?
- If you're home, can you focus on your loved ones, or are you unable to because you're still focused on your job?
- Can you name any of your hobbies, or are you unable to because work is your hobby?

If you want honest answers to these questions, consider asking your spouse or children what they think you should answer!

"Physician, Heal Thyself!"

I have difficulty sitting around. Even when I'm tired, I still feel the need to be productive. Katie has asked me many times: "Why do you always have to be working?" On the spectrum with workaholism on one side and laziness on the other, you can probably guess where I land.

In the last two weeks, I had an unexpected break from preaching. Whenever I don't have a sermon to prepare, my workload is considerably lighter. I wanted to use the extra time to finish this book. While writing this chapter (talk about God expecting me to walk-the-talk), Katie said, "You've been using so much of your free time to work on your book. I know you want to finish it, but why don't I make lunch for you and the kids, and you can go down to the lake to spend time with them?"

- The workaholic in me wanted to say, "I only have a few days left. Everything picks up again next week."
- The justifier in me wanted to say, "I can make up the time with the kids in the future. They'll understand."
- The spiritual hypocrite in me wanted to say, "I'm doing this for God. He wants me to get it done so I can help others and further His kingdom!"

I took my kids to the lake and had a wonderful time with them, but sadly these are the excuses I wanted to make. For me, pleasing God means resisting the temptation to put a book ahead of them. If we genuinely want to please the Lord, we must have our priorities in order.

The Consequences of Workaholism

Just as there are negative consequences to laziness, there are negative consequences to workaholism.

Physical Consequences
The Centers for Disease Control and Prevention published "Stress…At Work," and found that overworking increases the wear-and-tear on our bodies and contributes to headaches, back, and muscle pain.[xlv] There's an increase in blood pressure and the release of the hormone cortisol, which is hard on the heart and raises the risk for stroke, coronary artery disease, type 2 diabetes, and even cancer.[xlvi]

A 2010 study, "Overtime Is Bad for the Heart," published in the *European Heart Journal,* found working ten or more hours per day resulted in a 60 percent increase in cardiovascular issues.[xlvii] Many people have suffered heart attacks trying to climb the corporate ladder of success.

Emotional Consequences

A 2012 study, "Working Too Hard? Job Stress Doubles Depression Risk," suggests that those working long hours are twice as likely to experience a major depressive episode.[xlviii]

Another study, "Overtime Work as a Predictor of Major Depressive Episode," found that people working eleven hours per day can be over five times more likely to battle depression than those working seven to eight hours per day.[xlix]

Dr. Marianna Virtanen of the Finnish Institute of Occupational Health said, "Although occasionally working overtime may have benefits, it is important to recognize that working excessive hours is associated with an increased risk of major depression."[l]

Relationship Consequences

Workaholics don't invest an appropriate amount of time and energy in family and friends. Spouses, children, parents, and friends suffer because they recognize the workaholic's job is more important than a relationship with them. This can cause loved ones to become bitter and resentful. Many people have sacrificed their marriages and children for the next raise or promotion.

The fatigue and anxiety workaholics experience cause them to become irritable and impatient. Even when workaholics try to make time for others, the relationships still suffer because of their sour mood. Obsession with work affects not only the workaholic, but those close to them as well.

Performance Consequences

According to a 2014 study, "The Productivity of Working Hours," published by The Institute for the Study of Labor, people working seventy hours per week didn't accomplish more than their peers who worked fifty-six hours per week.[li] Why? Working too much causes productivity to suffer.

When people are unrested, their minds aren't as sharp, and they're more prone to make mistakes. Workaholism usually produces many things done mediocrely versus a few things done excellently.

Workaholics might strive to assist others by carrying more of the load, but they end up doing more harm than good because of the poor way they handle their responsibilities. This tends to frustrate the very people they're trying to help.

Spiritual Consequences

When we overwork, the only thing easier than neglecting our sleep, health, and family, is neglecting our relationships with the Lord. We're too busy to be active in the local church. Our involvement might be little more than irregular Sunday morning attendance. When the church offers events or opportunities to serve, we tell ourselves our work doesn't permit us to go.

We don't practice the spiritual disciplines. Prayer, time in the Word, and Scripture memorization take a backseat to our jobs. If we're workaholics, we probably can't remember the last time we sat down to pray or read the Bible for any length of time. When we reach the end of our lives, how much regret will we experience because of the time we invested in our jobs while neglecting God's kingdom?

The devil loves little more than distorting God's commands for us to work. He makes work so central to our lives that we become like hamsters running on wheels, and our relationship with the Lord is minimized, if not nonexistent. When Jesus taught the parable of the soils, He said, "Now he who received seed among the thorns is he who hears the word, and *the cares of this world and the deceitfulness of riches choke the word, and he becomes unfruitful*" (Matthew 13:22). Could there be a better picture of workaholism and its consequences? Workaholism is an obsession with the cares of this world. Workaholics are deceived into thinking riches are more important than their families and God. The spiritual is choked out, so they produce no fruit.

The Danger of Burnout

Burnout is an exhaustion that can be physical, emotional, social, spiritual, or any combination of these. People burnout when they're under great stress and overwhelming demands without adequate rest. Burnout can cause people to lose interest in relationships, hobbies, and even life in general.

There is nothing honorable about burning out for Jesus or anyone else. Sometimes burnout isn't the fault of a job or other people. It results when individuals work in one of the following ways:

- They exhaust themselves caring for others while failing to care for themselves.
- They neglect their needs in various ways, such as sacrificing sleep, over-extending their schedules, or failing to nourish themselves physically and spiritually.
- They excessively rely on themselves without relying on others.

Burnout can happen in:

- Businesses when individuals have ownership of plans or projects that should be distributed among team members
- Churches when people take on work that should be shared with brothers and sisters in Christ
- Families when people attempt to control the contentment or prosperity of parents, children, or spouses

Learning from the Mistake of a Great Leader

Perhaps the most evident instance of burnout in Scripture took place with Moses. Exodus 18:13 says, "Moses sat to judge the people; and the people stood before Moses from morning until evening." Moses thought he was doing a good thing, but when his father-in-law, Jethro, observed his behavior, he rebuked him: "The thing that you do is not good. Both you and these people who are with you will surely wear yourselves out. For this thing is too much for you; you are not able to perform it by yourself" (Exodus 18:17–18). The words "wear yourself out" are a concise description of burnout. Jethro rightly recognized Moses was doing too much. If Moses continued this approach, he and the people would suffer; therefore, Jethro counseled him:

> Moreover you shall select from all the people able
> men, such as fear God, men of truth, hating
> covetousness; and place such over them to be rulers
> of thousands, rulers of hundreds, rulers of fifties, and
> rulers of tens. And let them judge the people at all
> times. Then it will be that every great matter they shall
> bring to you, but every small matter they themselves
> shall judge. So it will be easier for you, for they will
> bear the burden with you. If you do this thing, and
> God so commands you, then you will be able to
> endure, and all this people will also go to their place in
> peace (Exodus 18:21–23).

What a wonderful picture of what should happen to prevent burnout! Let's take note of a few phrases:

- "It will be easier for you"—Moses was one of the greatest leaders in the Old Testament, but even he had to accept that he couldn't do everything. God gave Moses responsibility for the entire nation, but that didn't mean performing every task. There were lots of needs, but they didn't all belong to him. Likewise, regardless of the amount of authority we have, there can be lots of needs around us, but they don't all belong to us.

- "For they will bear the burden with you"—The solution was for Moses to delegate some of the responsibility to trustworthy, faithful people. The load had to be shared. This allowed others to participate in God's plan. Likewise, we often must delegate some responsibility—whether in the workplace, the home, or the church—to trustworthy, faithful people.

- "Then you will be able to endure"—In other words, "Then you won't burn out!" Moses was neglecting himself by overly relying on himself, which is a recipe for disaster. Delegating responsibility would give Moses longevity. Likewise, delegating is what we must do if we want to experience longevity.

- "And all this people will also go to their place in peace"— When Moses experienced burnout, he wasn't the only one affected. Thus, if he followed Jethro's advice, he wouldn't be the only one to benefit. Most of us have people depending on us. If we burnout, those around us will be affected. If we take care of ourselves, we won't be the only ones to benefit.

Learning from the Example of the Twelve Apostles

The twelve apostles acted in such a way it almost seems as though they looked back on Moses, learned from his mistake, and followed Jethro's advice. Acts 6:1 says, "Now in those days, when the number of the disciples was multiplying, there arose a complaint against the Hebrews by the Hellenists, because their widows were neglected in the daily distribution." The early church was growing exponentially. Earlier verses indicate three thousand and five thousand joined the church (Acts 2:41 and 4:4). John MacArthur said there could've been over 20,000 men and women.[lii] Regardless of the exact number, this was too many people for the Twelve to shepherd effectively.

The Hellenist widows said they weren't receiving a share of food, and this seemed to be a legitimate complaint. Acts 2:44–45 records the early church, "had all things in common, and sold their possessions and goods, and divided them among all, as anyone had need." Considering their generosity, more than likely, the neglect shown to the Hellenist widows was unintentional. There was simply a lack of oversight because the task was too big and the number of apostles was too small.

Resolving the situation would require considerable research and administration. The Twelve could've said, "We'll work harder! We need to make sure nobody falls through the cracks, especially not the widows. If we all put in a few more hours, we can get this under control." Instead, in Acts 6:2–4, they said:

> It is not desirable that we should leave the word of
> God and serve tables. Therefore, brethren, seek out
> from among you seven men of good reputation, full
> of the Holy Spirit and wisdom, whom we may appoint
> over this business; but we will give ourselves
> continually to prayer and to the ministry of the word.

This doesn't mean the Twelve didn't want to be waiters. This has nothing to do with serving the food or cleaning up after a meal. Instead, the word "tables" refers to tables for financial transactions. Think of Jesus turning over the moneychangers' tables.[1] In Luke 19:23, the same word is translated as "bank."

The Twelve didn't want to handle the administrative duties, such as distributing funds. It wasn't because they were lazy or thought it was beneath them. Instead, they wisely recognized they couldn't "serve tables" and fulfill the other responsibilities that God gave them. Taking care of widows is important (1 Timothy 5:3–16); but it can't take priority over the Word of God and prayer.

---

[1] See Matthew 21:12, Mark 11:15, and John 2:15.

Similarly, when we share responsibilities with others, it's not because we're lazy or we think it's beneath us. Instead, we recognize the load is too much for us. We have limited amounts of time and energy, and they're needed elsewhere.

Acts 6:5 says, "And the saying pleased the whole multitude. And they chose Stephen, a man full of faith and the Holy Spirit, and Philip, Prochorus, Nicanor, Timon, Parmenas, and Nicolas, a proselyte from Antioch." Guided by the Holy Spirit, they implemented the office of deacon to help with the ministry. God created the body of Christ with each member carrying some of the load:

- "*Bear one another's burdens*, and so fulfill the law of Christ" (Galatians 6:2).
- "From whom the whole body, joined and knit together by what every joint supplies, according to the effective working by which *every part does its share*, causes growth of the body for the edifying of itself in love" (Ephesians 4:16).
- "The manifestation of the Spirit is *given to each one* for the profit of all" (1 Corinthians 12:7).

We must recognize our limits. If we have more to do than we can handle, we must share the load with others. When the body of Christ works together, then all can rest in Christ.

Expect Negative Responses

Acts 6:5 says, "the whole multitude" was "pleased." This is the ideal result when sharing work with others, but there's no guarantee this will always be the case. It's best to assume setting boundaries and expecting others to carry some of the load will not go over well with some people.

If they are used to you always saying, "Yes," then they won't like your new approach. If you're the person in the workplace, community, or church who regularly "does everything," don't be surprised if people are displeased. Though you're doing what's best, they might complain, or accuse you of selfishness or laziness. It could even cost a relationship or two. Remember, this is a small price to pay in contrast to the even greater spiritual, emotional, physical, or mental price you'd pay from burnout.

Repenting of Workaholism

There are two categories of workaholics. The first category is made up of people who are thankful their jobs don't allow them to work less. They enjoy the excuse this gives them. They'd rather be at work, so they don't have to invest in their families or churches; therefore, they don't put forth any effort toward making appropriate changes. The sad truth is these people don't want to repent of workaholism.

The second category of workaholics want to repent, but they don't do so by swearing off work altogether. Instead, they make appropriate changes, which we can categorize as follows:

- Spiritually—They spend time praying, reading and meditating on the Word, listening to (or singing) Christian songs
- Emotionally—They seek counsel from church leaders or fellow Christians who can help them get things in perspective
- Relationally—They make time for friends, family, and fellowship, especially with those who refresh them
- Recreationally—They pursue hobbies and recreation they find to be life-giving, such as reading, journaling, drawing, cooking, or playing with children
- Physically—They get enough sleep, and take a day off (or two) and fill it with relaxing activities, such as walking, napping, or exercising

- Boundaries—They let the phone ring, put off responding to texts, leave the pile of work until the next day, and learn to say "No"
- Occupationally—They retire early, take a pay cut, or look for a new job

Since we know God doesn't want us to be workaholics, we can pray with confidence that He allows us to rest, have time for our families, and serve the church. I've seen God answer by providing a different schedule, a new boss, or an open door to another job. We should consult with Him before saying "Yes," and regularly ask Him to help us make the right choices and changes.

Putting Off Idolatry and Putting on Worship

If we let our relationship with work become sinful, there will be negative consequences for us and those around us. We must repent!

We should apply the principle of putting off and putting on. We put off the idolatry and put on heartfelt, grateful worship. Our love for Jesus trumps our love for our jobs. As we think of the work He did for us, we can't help but think less of the work we do throughout the week. Our jobs move from being idols, to occupying their rightful places as tools that allow us to serve Him.

Then we can rest. Developing a proper relationship with work means developing a proper relationship with rest. Working God's way also means resting God's way. In the following chapters, we'll learn the importance of resting, both physically and spiritually.

Chapter Thirteen

The Need for Physical Rest

On the surface, work and rest seem like opposites, as though one undoes the other. They appear to be mutually exclusive. To do one must mean that we reject doing the other. There's a conflict: do we work or rest? The answer is, yes! We're commanded to do both.

Rest is as much a theme from Genesis to Revelation as work. God introduced the concept of rest at creation. Genesis 2:2–3 says, "And on the seventh day God ended His work which He had done, and *He rested on the seventh day* from all His work which He had done. Then God blessed the seventh day and sanctified it, because in it *He rested from all His work* which God had created and made." God is omnipotent. He wasn't tired. He didn't need to rest. Instead, He was establishing a pattern for His people to follow.

The Ten Commandments made resting on the Sabbath a requirement of the Law. The fourth commandment in Exodus 20:8–11 reads:

> Remember the Sabbath day, to keep it holy. Six days you shall labor and do all your work, but the seventh day is the Sabbath of the LORD your God. In it you shall do no work: you, nor your son, nor your

daughter, nor your male servant, nor your female
servant, nor your cattle, nor your stranger who is
within your gates. For in six days the LORD made the
heavens and the earth, the sea, and all that is in them,
and rested the seventh day. Therefore the LORD
blessed the Sabbath day and hallowed it.

God said, "Remember the Sabbath," because it wasn't something
new; it had been around since creation. The command to rest was
not an excuse to be lazy, considering they had to work six full days
before the seventh. Since the Sabbath preceded the Mosaic Law, we
can "Remember the Sabbath to keep it holy" as a creation mandate.

Transition from the Seventh Day to First Day

Jesus and the disciples kept the fourth commandment, just as they
kept the other nine commandments. But there was a transition.

Jesus instituted the New Covenant at the Last Supper with these
familiar words: "This cup is the new covenant in My blood, which
is shed for you" (Luke 22:20). With the institution of the New
Covenant there was a shift from the seventh day of the week (the
Sabbath/Saturday) to the first day of the week (Sunday) in honor of
Christ's resurrection.[1] Thus, we see the first day of the week
emphasized in the New Testament. The phrase "first day of the
week" occurs eight times:

- Six times in the Gospels identifying the day of Jesus'
  resurrection: Matthew 28:1, Mark 16:2, 9, Luke 24:1, John
  20:1, and John 20:19

---

[1] With the transition from the Old Covenant to the New Covenant, Jesus
fulfilled the ceremonial portions of the Law, such as the sacrifices, circumcision,
and festivals. In Chapter Seventeen we'll discuss Jesus fulfilling the Sabbath.

- Once in Acts 20:7 identifying the day the early church met: "Now on the *first day of the week*, when the disciples came together to break bread" [2]
- Once when Paul encouraged believers to set aside something to give financially: "Now concerning the collection for the saints, as I have given orders to the churches of Galatia, so you must do also: On *the first day of the week* let each one of you lay something aside, storing up as he may prosper, that there be no collections when I come" (1 Corinthians 16:1-2). More than likely Paul told them to set their collections aside on the first day of the week, because that's when they gathered for worship.

If we only had Acts 20:7 stating the early church met on the first day of the week, this would be enough to encourage corporate worship on Sundays. Pastor John MacArthur writes, "The writings of the early church Fathers confirm the church continued to meet on Sunday after the close of the New Testament period."[liii] Matthew Henry writes, "The first day of the week is to be observed by all the disciples of Christ; and it is a sign between Christ and them."[liv]

While the first day of the week is emphasized in the New Testament, the seventh day (or Sabbath) is de-emphasized. The phrase "first day of the week" occurs eight times, but the phrase "seventh day of the week" never occurs. Understandably we'd expect the seventh day to be called, "Sabbath." The Sabbath is

---

[2] The words "break bread" refer to communion as opposed to simple fellowship together. The two are distinguished from each other in Acts 2:42: "And they continued steadfastly in the apostles' doctrine and *fellowship*, in the *breaking of bread*, and in prayers." As much as communion looks back to Christ's death, it also looks forward to His return: "For as often as you eat this bread and drink this cup, you proclaim the Lord's death till He comes" (1 Corinthians 11:26). They broke bread as part of their Sunday worship service. They wouldn't celebrate communion on the seventh day of the week when Jesus was resurrected on the first day of the week.

mentioned in the Gospels, but only because the transition to the first day of the week had not yet taken place. When the Sabbath is mentioned in Acts, it's associated with the practice of Jews who had not yet embraced Christ, but it's never associated with the practice or worship of the early church.

After Acts, the Sabbath only occurs in one verse: "So let no one judge you in food or in drink, or regarding a festival or a new moon or sabbaths, which are a shadow of things to come, but the substance is of Christ" (Colossians 2:16–17). After Acts, this is the only time the Sabbath is mentioned.

Since the epistles are the instruction letters for the church, it's inconceivable that there wouldn't be at least one verse commanding observing the Sabbath if that's what God wanted. Instead, Colossians 2:16–17, the one place mentioning the Sabbath, identifies it as a shadow pointing to Christ, and the command is for believers to avoid judging each other over their view of it and other nonessentials. We don't see any verses saying something similar for moral issues. In other words, there's no verse saying something like, "Let no one judge you regarding forgiveness, or love, or lying, or prayer, or service, or adultery." Unlike the Sabbath, these are moral issues involving judgment.

Similarly, Paul downplayed observing the Sabbath in Romans: "One person esteems one day above another; another esteems every day alike. Let each be fully convinced in his own mind. He who observes the day, observes it to the Lord; and he who does not observe the day, to the Lord he does not observe it" (Romans 14:5-6). Paul wouldn't write this if he wanted believers keeping the seventh day.

Although we aren't expected to keep the Sabbath under the New Covenant, we are expected to rest. Jesus said, "The Sabbath was made for man, and not man for the Sabbath" (Mark 2:27). Why would Jesus say this? Because we need to rest! Just as we are not at liberty to murder or commit adultery, we also are not at liberty to ignore the importance of rest.

The Need for Sleep

Sleep reveals that we are creatures, and not the Creator: "Behold, He who keeps Israel shall neither slumber nor sleep" (Psalm 121:4). Sleep reminds us of our limitations and the need to depend upon God for our very existence. This keeps us grateful and humble.

When God became a Man in the Person of Jesus Christ, He experienced our human limitations, including the need for rest. When Jesus left Judea for Galilee, He passed through Samaria and "being wearied from His journey, sat thus by the well" (John 4:6). At one point, He was so fatigued He slept in the bottom of a boat during a storm: "And suddenly a great tempest arose on the sea, so that the boat was covered with the waves. But He was asleep" (Matthew 8:24).

Mark 6:31 records Jesus' own words, "'Come aside by yourselves to a deserted place and *rest a while.*' For there were many coming and going, and they did not even have time to eat." Jesus and the disciples were so busy they didn't have time to eat, say nothing about sleep. Jesus was God in the flesh, and not a created being, yet He still sought time for Himself and the disciples to relax and refresh; therefore, we must see the same need in our lives.

We are weak. Our bodies require sleep to function and be recharged and refreshed. Sleep allows our minds to rest so we can think clearly when we wake. Lamentations 3:23 says, "[The Lord's mercies] are new every morning," implying that after a good night's sleep, we can pray for help and strength for the day. Sleep is a gift from God that we're wise to accept:

- "I will give peace in the land, and *you shall lie down*, and none will make you afraid" (Leviticus 26:6).

141

- "When *you lie down*, you will not be afraid; yes, *you will lie down* and *your sleep will be sweet*" (Proverbs 3:24).
- "I will both *lie down in peace, and sleep*; for You alone, O Lord, make me dwell in safety" (Psalm 4:8).

Conversely, the inability to sleep is presented negatively, often associated with fear and a guilty conscience:

- "I am weary with my groaning; all night I make my bed swim; I drench my couch with my tears" (Psalm 6:6).
- "You hold my eyelids open; I am so troubled that I cannot speak" (Psalm 77:4).
- "For they do not sleep unless they have done evil; and their sleep is taken away unless they make someone fall" (Proverbs 4:16).

The Consequences of Inadequate Sleep

Sleep is often neglected in our busy schedules. Some are inclined to view it as a luxury and think the benefit of a few more hours awake outweigh the negative consequences. Although scientists have only begun to identify the problems associated with insufficient sleep, enough studies have been performed that they agree the healthiest amount of sleep for adults is about seven to eight hours per night, and it's as important to health and well-being as nutrition and exercise.[lv]

While getting enough sleep does not guarantee good health, it does help vital functions. Many restorative functions take place during sleep, such as tissue repair, muscle growth, and protein synthesis. When we get enough sleep, we not only feel better but also increase the likelihood of living healthier, more productive lives. When we don't get enough sleep, there are considerable negative consequences.

142

Mortality

Researchers in the United Kingdom and Italy analyzed data from sixteen studies conducted over twenty-five years on more than 1.3 million people and more than one hundred thousand deaths. In 2010 the U.S. National Library of Medicine published their findings. The study, "Sleep Duration and All-Cause Mortality: A Systemic Review and Meta-Analysis of Prospective Studies," concluded people who sleep less than five to seven hours per night are 12 percent more likely to experience a premature death.[lvi]

The Institute of Medicine (US) Committee on Sleep Medicine and Research published another study: "Sleep Disorders and Sleep Deprivation: An Unmet Public Health Problem." They found that sleeping five or fewer hours per night may increase mortality risk by as much as 15 percent.[lvii]

Diabetes

God has designed our bodies so that during the deepest sleep the amount of glucose in our blood drops. In 2004, *Diabetes Care* published, "Incidence of Diabetes in Middle-Aged Men Is Related to Sleep Disturbances." The study found that improved sleep positively influences blood sugar control and reduces the likelihood of developing type 2 diabetes.[lviii]

On the other hand, another study, "Association of Sleep Time with Diabetes mellitus and Impaired Glucose Tolerance," found when we don't sleep enough, our bodies have a harder time responding to blood sugar levels, increasing the likelihood of developing type 2 diabetes.[lix] The *Archives of Internal Medicine* published the "Role of Sleep Duration and Quality in the Risk and Severity of Type 2 Diabetes Mellitus." The study found sleep deprivation can cause prediabetes in healthy adults in as little as six days.[lx]

Obesity

The Archives of Internal Medicine published, "Sleep Duration and Body Mass Index in a Rural Population." The study found people sleeping less than six hours per night are more likely to have excess body fat, while people sleeping eight hours per night had the lowest relative body fat.[lxi] Inadequate sleep negatively affects the hormones that regulate appetite. Levels of ghrelin, which stimulates appetite are increased, and levels of leptin, which suppresses appetite, are decreased. [lxii] Infants who sleep less are much more likely to develop obesity later in life than those who sleep longer.[lxiii]

Cardiovascular

While we sleep, our blood pressure decreases, allowing our hearts and blood vessels to rest.[lxiv] *The Journal of the American Medical Association* published, "Short Sleep Duration and Incident Coronary Artery Calcification." The study found that even moderately reducing sleep from eight hours per night to six or seven hours is associated with an increased risk of coronary artery calcification, which is a predictor of cardiovascular disease and heart attacks.[lxv]

Mental

The research aside, after a good night's sleep, most of us feel refreshed and energetic; after a poor night's sleep, we feel lethargic and fatigued. This affects us mentally. We lack motivation and initiative.

From a scientific standpoint, the Harvard Medical School published, "Sleep, Learning, and Memory." They found that the quantity and quality of sleep have a profound impact on learning and memory.[lxvi] Problem-solving skills and mental performance are also improved with adequate sleep.[lxvii]

Immune System

The U.S. National Library of Medicine published, "Partial Night Sleep Deprivation Reduces Natural Killer and Cellular Immune Responses in Humans." The study monitored the development of the common cold after giving people nasal drops with the cold virus. Researchers found that those who slept less than seven hours per night were almost three times more likely to develop a cold than those who slept eight hours or more.[lxviii] Another study, "Sleep Habits and Susceptibility to the Common Cold," found people who averaged less than seven hours of sleep per night were three times more likely to develop cold symptoms when exposed to the rhinovirus than those sleeping eight hours per night.[lxix]

Social

A Harvard University study revealed that our moods are negatively affected when we don't get adequate sleep.[lxx] When we're in a bad mood, we don't interact as well with others because we're typically more irritable. Another study, "Sleep Deprivation Impairs the Accurate Recognition of Human Emotions," used emotional facial recognition tests to find that people who hadn't slept well had greater difficulty recognizing others' emotional expressions. This hindered their relational skills because they couldn't recognize important social cues and process emotional information.[lxxi]

When Science Catches Up with Scripture

Why so many articles cited in the previous pages? Do we really need this research to tell us what to do? No, we don't. Having Scripture is enough; however, it's worth recognizing that academic articles support what God has commanded for centuries.

Millions of dollars go into studies, and they confirm the consequences of working too much, as well as the need for rest. God's commands are always for our benefit. Working too much and failing to rest is not "God's way."

The Spiritual Helps Us Rest Physically

Since rest is so important, how can we ensure we're resting enough? The best approach to this physical dilemma is found with a spiritual solution. Our relationships with the Lord allow us to rest when needed.

Rest Produced from Obeying the Lord

Since the Lord commands us to rest, if there was no other reason to do so, this should be enough. We set boundaries and train ourselves to rest, not necessarily because we feel like it, but because we want to obey. We trust the Lord knows best, and "Walk by faith, not by sight" (2 Corinthians 5:7). Rest is as much an issue of faith as every other area of the Christian life.

Rest Produced from the Lord's Leading

The Lord knows how much we can bear and when we should rest. We must prayerfully seek His schedule (versus our own) for our lives. But it's harder than ever in our loud, fast-paced culture that threatens to drown out God. The closer we are to Him, the more sensitive we are to His leading. The more our eyes are fixed on Jesus, the more likely we are to know when to rest, and the less likely we are to push through boundaries we should respect.

James 1:6 says, "Let him ask in faith, with no doubting, for he who doubts is like a wave of the sea driven and tossed by the wind." This language conjures up weary people who don't know what the Lord wants for them. If we're walking with Him, "we should no longer be children, tossed to and fro" (Ephesians 4:14). We're stable and unshifting, knowing what God does and doesn't want us to do.

Rest Produced from the Lord's Sovereignty

Nothing makes choosing to rest easier than knowing God is in control. We're liberated from worry and anxiety because we trust God will bring about the best end. We don't feel obligated to handle everything ourselves; instead, we are able to "Rest in the LORD, and wait patiently for Him" (Psalm 37:7).

"Relax" is a synonym for "rest." Sometimes the best way to rest is by relaxing our grip on our affairs and "casting all [our] care upon

Him, for He cares for [us]" (1 Peter 5:7).[3] Practically speaking, God's sovereignty allows us to:

- Head home on time, knowing He can take care of the work until the next day
- Decline the overtime, knowing He will provide for our needs
- Take a day off or go on vacation, knowing His will won't be thwarted by our absence
- Lie down at night and sleep soundly, knowing our lives are in His hands

Balance Is Required

One of the difficulties with laziness and workaholism is that they can't be handled with the severity Jesus commanded toward other sins. In Matthew 5:29–30, He said:

> If your right eye causes you to sin, pluck it out and cast it from you; for it is more profitable for you that one of your members perish, than for your whole body to be cast into hell. And if your right hand causes you to sin, cut it off and cast it from you; for it is more profitable for you that one of your members perish, than for your whole body to be cast into hell.

Jesus didn't expect us to do this literally. He often used figurative language, in the form of hyperbole, to make a point. In this case, He described the ruthlessness with which we should deal with sin. If we struggle with a certain temptation, we should completely remove (cut or pluck) it out of our lives. Show it no mercy:

---

[3] See also Psalm 55:22.

- People struggling with drunkenness throw away their alcohol.
- Men infatuated with sports cancel their cable television subscription.
- Women obsessed with shopping stay away from their favorite stores.
- Youths addicted to video games get rid of their gaming systems.

While this approach applies easily to some temptations, it's harder for others. For example:

- People struggling with gluttony don't cut food out of their lives.
- People struggling with laziness don't cut rest out of their lives.
- People struggling with workaholism don't cut work out of their lives.

If we think in think in terms of putting off and putting on, we don't put off laziness and put on workaholism, or put off workaholism and put on laziness. Instead, God wants us to have a strong work ethic, and He wants us to rest. We must ensure we don't:

- Give into laziness—rest too much, and fail to work enough
- Give into workaholism—work too much, and fail to rest enough

Simply put, balance is required! Regarding work, we depend on God for the strength we need to fulfill the responsibilities He's given us. We do the work He calls us to do with all our hearts, but we recognize boundaries are needed.

Regarding rest, we embrace it because that's what we need, and what God has commanded. We accept help from others because we can't do everything ourselves. We remember that our identity is not drawn from work we do, but from our relationship with Christ.

Along with resting physically, we must also rest spiritually, as we'll begin discussing in the following chapter!

Chapter Fourteen

The Importance of Resting at Jesus' Feet

The average foot contains six hundred sweat glands per square centimeter, which is hundreds more than the armpits.[lxxii] Our feet secrete salt, glucose, vitamins, and amino acids that provide the perfect diet for bacteria to thrive. In appreciation for the food, bacteria leave us with fatty acids that produce the common foot odor. Given our anatomy, no matter how clean we are, foot odor is almost unavoidable.

Feet might smell bad in our day, but we can be sure they smelled even worse in Jesus' day. While most of us don't like the idea of being too close to people's feet, Mary didn't let it hold her back. Luke 10:38–42 records:

> Now it happened as they went that He entered a certain village; and a certain woman named Martha welcomed Him into her house. And she had a sister called Mary, who also sat at Jesus' feet and heard His word. But Martha was distracted with much serving, and she approached Him and said, "Lord, do You not care that my sister has left me to serve alone? Therefore tell her to help me."

> And Jesus answered and said to her, "Martha, Martha, you are worried and troubled about many things. But one thing is needed, and Mary has chosen that good part, which will not be taken away from her."

The village is Bethany, which was about two miles east of Jerusalem on the slope of the Mount of Olives. Mary and Martha were sisters, and their brother was Lazarus, whom Jesus raised from the dead. More than likely, all three of them lived together in this house. Mary shows up three times in Scripture, and each time she's at Jesus' feet.[1] When Jesus arrived, the sisters responded differently: Mary sat at the Lord's feet, listening to His teaching, and Martha was "distracted with much serving."

While it's easy to condemn Martha, let's put ourselves in her place. She has Jesus—the Christ, the Lord, the Son of God—for dinner. She "welcomed Him into her house" and wanted everything to be perfect. She's busy with all the food preparations and formalities that we would expect. All the while, her sister, Mary, seemed to be relaxing! Would you be frustrated if you were Martha? Mary lived under the same roof. She should have felt equally responsible for making sure things went well, but she seemed to be doing nothing more than sitting idly at Jesus' feet.

How do we explain Martha being rebuked, and Mary being commended? Making it more striking, Martha was serving Jesus! It would be one thing if she were serving someone else, but she was serving the Lord!

Devotion Is More Important than Service

Unfortunately, people contrast Mary and Martha and teach that Christians must make a choice: be a worshiper like Mary or a servant

---

[1] See also John 11:32 and John 12:3.

like Martha. They think it's "either/or" when it's actually both: we should be worshipers *and* servants. What do we hope to hear when we stand before the Lord? "Well done good and faithful person who sat at Jesus' feet" or "Well done good and faithful person who prayed and read the Bible every day." No. We hope to hear, "Well done good and faithful servant" (Matthew 25:21, 23). This account is not minimizing service. Instead, it is elevating devotion.

"Martha was distracted with much serving," but distracted from whom, or from what? From Jesus and His teaching! She was so busy with excessive preparations for Jesus; she ended up neglecting Him. She brought Him into her home but then didn't give Him the attention He deserves. Warren Wiersbe said, "What we do with Jesus is more important than what we do for Him."[lxxiii] God is more interested in our spiritual relationship with Him than He is in our physical service for Him: "For I desire mercy (relationship) and not sacrifice (service), and the knowledge of God (relationship) more than burnt offerings (service)" (Hosea 6:6).

We know what it looked like two thousand years ago for Mary to sit at Jesus' feet and listen to His teaching, but what does it look like for us today?

- Committing time each day to praying and reading God's Word
- Meditating on Jesus' words and listening to Him with an open heart and mind
- Imitating Mary's example and making our devotional time a priority over other things, even good things, such as serving
- Learning from Martha's example and removing things that distract us from focusing on the Lord

We must make every effort to sit at Jesus' feet and enjoy Him, rather than miss Him like Martha did because she was fussing over the details. Martha focused on the physical, but Mary focused on the spiritual. The food and dishes are temporary, but Jesus is eternal.

Sitting at Jesus' Feet Is a Choice

We misunderstand Mary and Martha if we think they're two people simply living out their different personalities. We say, "Martha is a servant, so she served, and Mary is a worshiper, so she worshiped." The problem is this gives the impression Mary's not a servant, but Martha said, "My sister *has left me* to serve alone." Mary had been serving too; she didn't sit at Jesus' feet because she was lazy.

Jesus said, "Martha, Martha, you are worried and troubled about many things. But one thing is needed, and Mary has chosen that good part, which will not be taken away from her." Jesus rebuked Martha and then commended Mary, but what did Mary actually *do* that deserved a commendation? It looks like she did nothing! She was a silent example to her sister. She modeled what to do by not doing anything. Sometimes silence can be a great example (or rebuke) to others.

The account is set up in such a way that Mary and Martha's situations are identical. They live in the same house. Jesus came into the house that belonged to them both. They were both serving. They both faced the same choice: keep serving or sit at Jesus' feet. Jesus said Mary "[chose] that good part," and that's why He commended her. Mary could've been doing other things, but she chose to sit at Jesus' feet. Mary worshiped, not because she was naturally a worshiper and acted according to her personality, but because that's what she chose.

Choosing the Better

In the NKJV Jesus said, "Mary has chosen the good part," but the NIV says she "has chosen *what is better*." Often the Christian life consists of choosing, not just between good and evil, but between good and better. Martha didn't choose something bad or spiritually neutral. She chose something that is good—serving! But at this moment, sitting at Jesus' feet and listening to Him was better than serving Him. Service is good, but devotion is better.

Our lives are busy. We have jobs, homes, children, responsibilities, schoolwork, and chores that pull on our time and energy. We also only have twenty-four hours in each day, and we must choose how we're going to spend those hours and what we're going to prioritize. When people choose to spend time at Jesus' feet, it's not because they have more time available, or because their lives are easier or less hectic. Instead, it's because they made sitting at Jesus' feet a priority. Conversely, when people don't spend time at Jesus' feet, it's not because they don't have time, or because their lives are harder and busier. Instead, it's because they had other priorities.

Sometimes people don't sit at Jesus' feet, and then they say, "I didn't have the time." Typically, this is a lie because they were able to find time for other things they wanted to do. We make time for the things that are most important to us. Mary had all the competitions for her time and energy that Martha had, but she chose to put Jesus first. She made everything else—even serving—second.

At least occasionally, all of us have resembled Martha more than Mary. We rush around doing "what needs to be done," while missing the glimpses of Jesus all around us. As difficult as it is, and as contrary to our culture as it is, we must intentionally try to slow down and model Mary.

Avoiding Rebukes from Jesus

Considering what happened in Luke 10, something interesting took place less than one year later in John 12:1–8:

> Then, six days before the Passover, Jesus came to
> Bethany, where Lazarus was who had been dead,

155

whom He had raised from the dead. There they made
Him a supper; and *Martha served*, but Lazarus was one
of those who sat at the table with Him. Then *Mary
took a pound of very costly oil of spikenard, anointed the feet of
Jesus, and wiped His feet* with her hair. And the house
was filled with the fragrance of the oil.
But one of His disciples, Judas Iscariot, Simon's son,
who would betray Him, said, "Why was this fragrant
oil not sold for three hundred denarii and given to the
poor?" This he said, not that he cared for the poor,
but because he was a thief, and had the money box;
and he used to take what was put in it.
But Jesus said, "Let her alone; she has kept this for the
day of My burial. For the poor you have with you
always, but Me you do not have always."

This is the day before Jesus' Triumphal Entry and less than one
week before His crucifixion. Martha prepared a meal for Jesus, the
Twelve, her brother, and her sister. That's fifteen people! They ate
while reclining at the table with their feet extended away from them.
This allowed Mary to perform the act that symbolized her devotion
to her Savior. A denarius is one day's wage, so the spikenard was
approximately one year's wages.[2] There are several similarities
between this account and the previous account with Mary and
Martha:

- Jesus is in the home of Mary, Martha, and Lazarus again.
- Mary is at Jesus' feet again, engaging in another act of devotion.
- Martha is serving again.
- Jesus is pleased with Mary's behavior again.

---

[2] The spikenard was worth three hundred denarii. People earned money about three hundred days per year since they didn't work on Sabbaths or holy days.

- Jesus defends Mary's behavior again (previously to Martha and now to Judas).

Since Martha is serving again and Mary is at Jesus' feet again, what else would we expect? We would expect Jesus to rebuke Martha again, but this is one of the main differences from the previous account. He didn't for two important reasons.

Jesus Didn't Rebuke Martha Because She Didn't Have Something Better to Choose

In this account, Jesus was eating, but He wasn't teaching. It was an appropriate time for Martha to serve. In Luke 10:42, Jesus said, "One thing is needed, and Mary has chosen that good part." The "one thing needed" was listening to Jesus, and "Mary [chose] that "good part," but now there was nothing better to choose.

John 12:3 says, "The house was filled with the fragrance of [the perfume]." I'm sure everyone loved the way the room smelled, but soon everyone would be hungry, and then they'd love the smell of the food Martha cooked. Serving might not look as extravagant as pouring perfume on Jesus' feet, but it's invaluable.

The account in John 10 focuses on what Mary did because it was a beautiful act of devotion and worship—although serving is also a beautiful act of devotion and worship! Jesus said, "Just as the Son of Man did not come to be served, but to serve, and to give His life a ransom for many" (Matthew 20:28). Jesus was such a servant that few things in life resemble Jesus as much as serving. This fact alone makes serving beautiful and extravagant.

Jesus Didn't Rebuke Martha Because She Served with the Right Heart

In the previous account, Jesus rebuked Martha in front of many people, which must have been very humbling. Martha did two things to her credit. First, she didn't pout or quit. She could've said, "Forget it. I try to serve, but nobody appreciates it. I even get rebuked. I'm never serving again." Instead, she went back to serving!

Second, she learned from what took place earlier. The account says, "Martha served," but who else served? We know Mary didn't, because she was busy pouring perfume on Jesus' feet. There's no indication anybody else served, which is to say nobody helped Martha. What's different about her this time? Her attitude! She's serving with a joyful heart. The Lord wants us serving, but He cares how that service is performed.

One of the keys to working and resting God's way is knowing when to do one or the other. We must find the right balance between the two in our busy lives if we're going to be healthy physically, mentally, emotionally, and spiritually. Sometimes the rest we need is physical, while other times, it is spiritual. We've already discussed resting physically. In the next chapter, we'll discuss resting spiritually. Sometimes the best way to serve Jesus is simply by sitting at His feet.

Chapter Fifteen

When We Must Sit at Jesus' Feet

Mary's posture at Jesus' feet stands in stark contrast to churches that neglect the one thing needed. Willow Creek has been one of America's most influential churches. They had elaborate programs and activities, and the measure of success was the number of people serving. So they thought. But then they conducted a thorough, multiple-year study of their ministry and found their programs and activities didn't produce spiritual growth. Bill Hybels was the senior pastor at the time, and to his credit, he was open about their findings:

> Some of the stuff that we have put millions of dollars into thinking it would really help our people grow and develop spiritually, when the data actually came back, it wasn't helping people that much. Other things that we didn't put that much money into and didn't put much staff against is stuff our people are crying out for. We made a mistake. What we should have done when people crossed the line of faith and become Christians, we should have started telling people and teaching people that they have to take responsibility to become self-feeders. We should have gotten people, taught people, how to read their Bible between

service, how to do the spiritual practices much more aggressively on their own.[lxxiv]

They found that keeping people busy had not produced sanctification. The church of Sardis demonstrates the same. In Jesus' letter to the church, He said, "These things says He who has the seven Spirits of God and the seven stars: 'I know your works, that you have *a name that you are alive, but you are dead*'" (Revelation 3:1). They had "a name" or reputation that they were "alive," which means they were known as the happening church.

The people were busy, but Jesus said they were dead. How can a church be alive and dead? They were alive (and busy) physically, but dead spiritually. It's an unbelievably sad irony that the church everyone thought was thriving was filled with unregenerate people.

Sitting at Jesus' Feet Sanctifies, but Service Might Not

Jesus told the Twelve to make disciples by "teaching them to observe all things that I have commanded you" (Matthew 28:20). Disciples need to receive Jesus' teaching, and Mary received His teaching directly from Him, at His feet!

Willow Creek incorrectly thought programs produce spiritual growth. The word of Christ alone produces spiritual growth:

- "Sanctify them by Your truth. Your word is truth" (John 17:17).
- "[Christ] might sanctify and cleanse [the church] with the washing of water by the word" (Ephesians 5:26).
- "As newborn babes, desire the pure milk of the word, that you may grow thereby" (1 Peter 2:2).

The Word equips us to live out the Christian life:

> All Scripture is given by inspiration of God, and is profitable for doctrine, for reproof, for correction, for instruction in righteousness, that the man of God may be complete, thoroughly equipped for every good work (2 Timothy 3:16–17).

Ephesians 4:12 says church leaders are supposed to "[equip] the saints for the work of the ministry," and if saints are equipped by God's Word, then church leaders need to feed their flocks the word. God's Word gives us faith: "So then faith comes by hearing, and hearing by the word of God" (Romans 10:17). Faith comes from the Word because we can't have faith in a God we don't know, and we know God through His Word; through sitting at the feet of Jesus.

Considering where the account of this episode with Mary and Martha appears is instructive. Luke 10:1–24 records the sending of the Seventy, which is about the preaching of the gospel. Luke 10:25–37 records the Good Samaritan, which is about serving one's neighbor. Mary and Martha follow in Luke 10:38–41, revealing that before we can do either of the aforementioned—preach the gospel or serve—we must first spend time with Jesus. Why? He alone fuels our ministry. Physical effort can never accomplish what must be done in the Spirit. We can't rise above our relationships with the Lord. Jesus Himself said, "I am the vine, you are the branches. He who abides in Me, and I in him, bears much fruit; for without Me you can do nothing" (John 15:5).

When we try to serve the Lord, but we haven't sat at His feet, it can be damaging. Few things are as harmful as people trying to serve Jesus when they haven't spent time with Him. Consider Martha's example. Time at Jesus' feet is what she needed more than anything else. We tend to think service benefits us, but Martha, Willow Creek, and Sardis show us that's not always the case! In Martha's case, her Christless service revealed her resentful, proud, and crabby heart.

161

The Problems with Being Overwhelmed

The Greek word for "distracted" is *perispao*, and it means "over-occupied" or "too busy."[lxxv] Martha was overwhelmed. You can picture her turning from one task to the next, fussing over all the details: ensuring the table is set, the food is served at the right time, and everyone is comfortable. Ironically, her fussing probably made people uncomfortable. She was driven by circumstances and pulled in too many directions. Not only did she take on more than she could handle, but she also took on tasks the Lord didn't even want. She was making elaborate preparations, ostensibly for the Lord, but they were not the one thing needed.

This is fitting for us because we live in a fast-paced culture. There's no end to the number of things we can do or distractions that can pull us in. If we're not careful, we find ourselves overwhelmed. We become like Martha taking on things Jesus might not want us doing, or that might pale in comparison to what He would rather we do. My wife, Katie, has a wise perspective here, and I appreciate her humility in sharing this:

> I have a tendency to put too much on my plate. I remember doing this in college when I worked three jobs and went to school full-time. When I married Scott, he witnessed this firsthand. I was often overwhelmed, so he encouraged me to focus on the tasks the Lord put in front of me—homeschooling our children and keeping the home. Even though I hate boundaries I know they are instruments of peace for me. I want to encourage any Marthas reading this to seek your husband's counsel before signing up for something. We certainly don't want our families suffering because we are too busy.

The account with Mary and Martha follows the Good Samaritan, which is one of the most convicting accounts in Scripture regarding serving. Then we reach Martha and learn an important lesson—

service must be done the right way. Galatians 5:22 lists peace as a fruit of the Spirit. Since Martha didn't have peace, we may rightly conclude that she was serving in the flesh, not in the Spirit.

One problem with being overwhelmed is it often introduces sins into our lives. When we're stressed, or when we've taken on more than we can handle, we're faced with many temptations. This happened to Martha, and she gave in. The feet of Jesus was the one place in all the world she should've been. By looking at her example we can see when we must sit at Jesus' feet.

We Must Sit at Jesus' Feet When We Are Filled with Self-Pity
Martha said to Jesus, "Lord, do You not care that my sister has left me to serve alone?" She thought she was being neglected and overlooked, so she felt sorry for herself. She thought nobody cared about her and all that she had to do.

The same thing can happen with us. We feel like we're the only ones working, we must do everything ourselves, and nobody cares about us. When we find ourselves filled with self-pity, we must examine our hearts and see whether we're serving with the right attitude.

A good test is whether we have joy. If we don't, what is the solution? The solution is *not* to quit working. Having a pity party isn't an excuse to avoid serving. We don't put off a bad attitude by putting on laziness. The solution is to take steps to have a better attitude, and that means spending time at Jesus' feet until we can serve Him and others joyfully.

We Must Sit at Jesus' Feet When We Are Easily Annoyed
Martha said, "My sister has left me to serve alone." You can imagine her giving Mary dirty looks, stomping around, sighing, huffing and puffing, maybe even slamming dishes, hoping someone notices. She became more and more upset until she finally did something we wouldn't believe if it wasn't recorded—she interrupted Jesus while He was teaching!

We should believe she did this, though, because we do the same thing when we are not fixing our eyes on Jesus and sitting at His feet. We interrupt Him with our complaining spirit, arguments, and disobedience when He's teaching us hard lessons.

Martha wasn't upset about serving. For people like her, rarely will service itself be the point of annoyance. Instead, service is their element; it's what they enjoy. The annoyance will come from others who don't pitch in. This can happen to us too. We feel like we're the only ones serving, which leads us to be annoyed with those around us. When we're impatient, agitated, resentful, rude, bossy, controlling, or insensitive in our service, these are signs we need to sit at Jesus' feet.

Sometimes a husband comes home from working hard all day, and he's easily annoyed with his wife or children. Sometimes a wife is having a bad day, so she's going to make sure the rest of her family has a bad day too. Psalm 127:3 says, "Behold, children are a heritage from the LORD, the fruit of the womb is a reward." Sometimes children seem like they're doing everything they can to disprove this verse. If we're men, women, or children, and we find ourselves acting like this, we need to spend time at Jesus' feet.

We Must Sit at Jesus' Feet When We Are Frustrated with the Lord

Martha said, "Lord, do You not care that my sister has left me to serve alone?" Martha wasn't only annoyed with others. She was frustrated with Jesus! This was a strong criticism: "You don't care about me, or all I'm going through, or that my sister is being lazy. You're just letting her sit there!" She thought Jesus was unjust, so she told Him what He could do to be just: "Tell her to help me!" This was an order! Keep in mind Jesus was in the middle of teaching! She interrupted, accused, and ordered.

Sometimes we can feel like the Lord doesn't care about us, our circumstances, or the load we're under. When we start feeling this way, it's a clear sign we need to spend time at His feet. Why? Martha became upset with Jesus because she didn't understand why He didn't care about her, why He would let her do all the work, why He wouldn't tell Mary to help her. Often when we're upset with the Lord, it's because we don't understand why He is:

- Allowing certain circumstances in our lives
- Letting things be so difficult for us
- Making us do things other people don't have to do

When we experience this type of confusion, we must sit at Jesus' feet. This isn't to say all our questions will be answered, but we'll be given the peace needed to accept our circumstances.

If we've sinned against the Lord through our attitude, we must also repent! Job was confused by his suffering. He complained, accused, and demanded:

> *I will not restrain my mouth*; I will speak in the anguish of my spirit; *I will complain* in the bitterness of my soul…Then call, and I will answer; or let me speak, then *You respond to me*…As for me, *is my complaint against man?* And if it were, *why should I not be impatient?* Oh, *that the Almighty would answer me,* that my Prosecutor had written a book! (Job 7:11, 13:22, 21:4, 31:35).[1]

Job was frustrated with the Lord! God finally responded. Instead of answering any of Job's questions, God chose to ask Job seventy-seven questions that demonstrate His greatness (Job 38:1–40:2). Job responded, "Behold, *I am vile*; what shall I answer You? I lay my hand over my mouth. Therefore I have uttered what I did not understand, things too wonderful for me, which I did not know.

---

[1] See also Job 3:26, 4:2–16, 6:24, 21:5–17.

Therefore I abhor myself, and *repent in dust and ashes*" (Job 40:4, 42:3, 6).

To Job's credit, he said he was "vile," and he repented of his criticisms. Martha also needed to repent of accusing Jesus of being uncaring. If we have sinned through our words or in our hearts, we must repent too.

We Must Sit at Jesus' Feet When We Are Anxious

Jesus graciously responded: "Martha, Martha, you are worried and troubled about many things." One of the difficulties with Scripture is the same difficulty we have with emails and letters—the tone is hard to convey! We must guess how people are trying to "sound." Sometimes they put words in uppercase or add multiple exclamation points to make it "sound" like they're yelling. The same is true in this account. We must guess how Martha spoke to Jesus and how Jesus responded to Martha. Martha was demanding. Perhaps she yelled at Jesus, but I suspect Jesus responded tenderly. She was upset with Him, but He was gentle with her.

He didn't rebuke her for working and serving, but He did rebuke her worry. Philippians 4:6 says, "Be anxious for nothing," and this includes anxiety over even seemingly good things such as making preparations for others. If you've ever been in a leadership position, you know how much you want to see things go well. It's tempting to be filled with anxiety: "What if I don't get everything finished? What if I forget something?"

Martha was troubled by preparations she thought needed to be made, and in the moment, they seemed like a big deal. A spiritual, eternal perspective reveals all these physical, temporal details are small. It's one thing to be concerned about unsaved people going to hell, the spiritual health of the church, God's name being blasphemed, or unity among brothers and sisters in Christ. Martha was worried about ordinary matters with little-to-no eternal consequence.

When we're filled with anxiety, is it typically over issues with eternal consequences? Perhaps. I'd guess, however, more times than not, we're filled with anxiety over considerably less important issues. Sitting at Jesus' feet gives us the spiritual perspective we need.

We Must Sit at Jesus' Feet When We Are Worried About Others

In Matthew 6:25, Jesus said, "Do not worry," and then He used the word "worry" five more times in verses 27–34. Some worry seems reasonable, such as when waiting for a diagnosis from the doctor. In Martha's case, she was worried about what her sister was and wasn't doing, which is unreasonable.

After Jesus' resurrection, He met with the disciples and told Peter how he would die. John 21:18, 20–22 records:

> [Jesus said], "Most assuredly, I say to you, when you were younger, you girded yourself and walked where you wished; but when you are old, you will stretch out your hands, and another will gird you and carry you where you do not wish."
> Then Peter, turning around, saw [John and] said to Jesus, "But Lord, *what about this man?*"
> Jesus said to him, "If I will that he remain till I come, *what is that to you? You follow Me.*"

After Peter learned he would experience a painful death, he wanted to know what would happen with the other disciples, in particular, John. Jesus basically told him, "Don't worry about him. Just worry about yourself."

We can spend time and energy worrying about others, but not always in a good way. Social media has made this problem worse. We get windows into people's lives that allow us to follow their marriages, children, trips, activities, meals, and it's not always a good thing. We judge people's actions, decisions, relationships, the ways they spend their time and money. When this happens, we need to sit at Jesus' feet, because He helps us "worry" more about ourselves.

Let me back up a little to get some momentum into the rest of this point. The world wants to blur the lines between the genders. They've moved past denying that men and women have different roles and responsibilities to teach that there aren't even men and women anymore: a man can be a woman, and a woman can be a man. Christians need to hold to the plain teaching of Genesis 1:27 that "He created them male and female" and there are differences.[2]

Part of the differences is that some temptations are more common to one gender than the other. For example:

- "Husbands, love your wives, and do not be harsh with them" (Colossians 3:19 ESV). Since husbands are mentioned and there's no corresponding verse telling wives not to be harsh with their husbands, this seems to be a temptation that's stronger for men than women.
- "Fathers, do not provoke your children to wrath" (Ephesians 6:4). This isn't to say mothers can't provoke their children, but since this is said to fathers without a corresponding verse for mothers, this seems to be a greater temptation for men than for women.

For wives, 1 Peter 3:1 commands them to "win over their husbands without a word," and six verses in Proverbs discuss them nagging their husbands.[3] While men can struggle with nagging, without corresponding verses telling them not to nag their wives, this seems to indicate that nagging is a greater tendency for women than for men.

---

[2] See also Genesis 5:2, Mark 10:6, and Matthew 19:4.

[3] Proverbs 19:13, 21:9, 19, 25:24, 27:15–16.

First Timothy 5:13 says some women "learn to be idle, wandering about from house to house, and not only idle but also gossips and busybodies, saying things which they ought not." Men can be gossips and busybodies, but since Paul directs this teaching to women, it suggests that gossip is generally a stronger tendency for women than for men. Martha seemed to succumb to the temptation to see the speck in her sister's eye more than the beam in her own.

Ladies reading this should examine themselves and consider whether they spend too much time and energy worrying about the perceived sins of others. If that's the case, look at Jesus' words to Martha, but substitute your own name: "Sarah, Sarah, you are worried and troubled about many things." Would Jesus say this to you?

Most of the women I know have a lot on their plates. They're busy with their husbands, children, homes, and churches. Worrying less about the behavior of others should be viewed as a blessing!

A Supernatural Solution

Calling out to the Lord for help is a theme in Scripture, but there's a right and wrong way to do it. The psalmist called out the right way:

- "In my distress *I called upon the* LORD, *and cried out to my God; He heard my voice* from His temple, and my cry came before Him, even to His ears" (Psalm 18:6).
- "*I sought the* LORD, *and He heard me*, and delivered me from all my fears" (Psalm 34:4).
- "*I called on the* LORD *in distress; the Lord answered me* and set me in a broad place" (Psalm 118:5).

When the Israelites were in the wilderness, they repeatedly called out for help the wrong way: "The people complained against Moses, saying, 'What shall we drink?'" (Exodus 15:24) and "[They] yielded to intense craving; so the children of Israel wept again and said: 'Who will give us meat to eat?'" (Numbers 11:4).[4] Martha also called out to the Lord the wrong way.

Rather than being like Martha or Israel in the wilderness, we shouldn't grumble and complain. Instead, we should pray humbly with child-like faith trusting that our heavenly Father will help us.

Self-pity, annoyance, frustration, anxiety, and worry are spiritual issues; therefore, the solution for them must be spiritual and supernatural, versus earthly and natural. Sitting at Jesus' feet is the remedy for the above temptations. When we have a bad attitude and recognize it needs to change, if we don't spend time with Jesus, we'll end up like Martha: busy, but not blessed. She is a great example of the many consequences of working too much and with the wrong attitude.

---

[4] See also Exodus 14:11, 16:2, 17:2–3, Numbers 11:1, 14:2, Psalm 106:25, and 1 Corinthians 10:10.

Chapter Sixteen

The Promised Land and Spiritual Rest

John Eliot was a Puritan missionary to the American Indians, pastor of the First Church in Roxbury, and founder of the Roxbury Latin School in the Massachusetts Bay Colony. He fulfilled his pastoral duties, including preaching biweekly into his eighties, while ministering to the Indians. He took up court cases for their property rights, pleaded for clemency for them, fought against them being sold into slavery, sought to secure lands and streams for their use, and established schools for them. He labored to consolidate Indians so they could enjoy a Christian society, and at one point, there were fourteen towns of "Praying Indians." Eliot learned their tongue so he could translate sermon transcripts, the Bible, and twenty other books into their language.[lxxvi]

Eliot was busier than most of us can imagine. He seemed as though he lived the lives of many men. Why do many of God's most faithful servants work the hardest, and yet are rested and at peace? The answer is there's a rest that's not physical. The most important rest is spiritual, and they experience it. Conversely, why do some of the laziest people, who do the least, seem overwhelmed and filled

171

with anxiety? They experience physical rest, but they lack spiritual rest.

The clearest passage explaining spiritual rest is Hebrews 3:7–4:11. Rest is the theme of the verses as the word occurs twelve times. The author of Hebrews also references the Old Testament extensively in these verses. Unfortunately, sometimes people read the Old Testament and think, "What does this have to do with me? How can I learn from people who lived so long ago and whose lives are so different from mine?" These are unfortunate questions because the New Testament states the Old Testament provides us with examples and instruction:

- "For whatever things were written [in the Old Testament] were written for our learning" (Romans 15:4).
- "Now all these things happened to [the Israelites] as examples, and they were written for our admonition" (1 Corinthians 10:11).

Often, the Old Testament provides a backdrop for New Testament instruction. One such example takes place as the author of Hebrews reveals that the Promised Land is a type and shadow of the spiritual rest God offers His people.

We must be familiar with Israel's rebellion on the border of the Promised Land. In Numbers 13 and 14, the twelve spies returned after spending forty days examining the land. They shared their report with the nation, that while the land was as wonderful as God said, it was also filled with enemies. Ten of the spies said Israel couldn't defeat the enemies, but Joshua and Caleb said God would give them victory.

Tragically, the people believed the ten spies, so they didn't believe God; therefore, God said the nation couldn't enter. They would've received the land the next day, which means what was about to be a wonderful blessing for them, ended up being a moment of historic discipline. Israel was forced to wander in the wilderness for forty years—one year for each day the spies were in the land (Numbers 14:34). The generation of unbelief would die, but their children, whom they accused God of trying to murder, would enter the land (Numbers 14:3 cf. Numbers 14:31).

The author of Hebrews has this rebellion in view as he presents the Promised Land as a picture of spiritual rest. We will consider this passage piece by piece throughout this chapter.

An Urgent Matter

> Therefore, as the Holy Spirit says: "Today, if you will hear His voice" (Hebrews 3:7).

Psalm 95 records the rebellion as God saw it, and the author of Hebrews quotes Psalm 95:7–11 in Hebrews 3:7–11. Although Psalm 95 was written by David as a wonderful affirmation of the inspiration of Scripture, it is attributed to the Holy Spirit. David was the human author, but the Holy Spirit is the true and greater Author of all of God's Word.

To convey urgency, this is the first of four times the author uses the word "Today."[1] Don't put off entering God's rest! Live as though you might not have the same opportunity tomorrow. The Israelites serve as a warning to us. They were to enter the Promised Land, but they rebelled and were told they couldn't enter (Numbers 14:1–4). They attempted to enter but were chased out by the Canaanites (Numbers 14:39–45).

---

[1] Also in Hebrews 3:13, 15, and 4:7.

Unbelief Is a Heart Issue

> Do not harden your hearts as in the rebellion (or at
> Meribah, which means, "tempting or testing"), in the
> day of trial (or at Massah, which means, "contention
> or quarreling") in the wilderness, where your fathers
> tested Me, tried Me, and saw My works forty years.
> Therefore I was angry with that generation, and said,
> 'They always go astray in their heart, and they have
> not known My ways' (Hebrews 3:8–10).

This is the first of three times the warning, "Do not harden your
hearts" occurs.[2] The author holds them responsible for their
unbelief because belief and unbelief are not independent of people's
will. This is the first of four times the heart is mentioned because
belief and unbelief are heart issues: "For with the heart one believes"
(Romans 10:10).[3] Hence, "They always go astray in their heart."

"Tested" and "tried" describe Israel's behavior in the wilderness,
and it is always related to their unbelief.

- They didn't believe God would deliver them from the
  Egyptian army: "When Pharaoh drew near, [Israel] said to
  Moses, 'Because there were no graves in Egypt, have you
  taken us away to die in the wilderness? Why have you so dealt
  with us, to bring us up out of Egypt?'" (Exodus 14:10–11).
- They didn't believe God would provide water for them:
  "[Israel] complained against Moses, saying, 'What shall we
  drink?'" (Exodus 15:24) and "[Israel] contended with Moses,
  'Give us water, that we may drink'" (Exodus 17:2).
- They didn't believe God would provide food for them:
  "Israel complained against Moses and Aaron in the

---

[2] Also in Hebrews 3:15 and 4:7.

[3] Also in Hebrews 3:10, 3:12, and 3:15.

wilderness [saying], 'Oh, that we had died by the hand of the LORD in the land of Egypt, when we sat by the pots of meat and when we ate bread to the full! For you have brought us out into this wilderness to kill this whole assembly with hunger'" (Exodus 16:2–3).

- They didn't believe God appointed Moses as their leader: "[Israel] said, 'Has the LORD indeed spoken only through Moses? Has He not spoken through us also?'" (Numbers 12:2).

When God is "tested and [tried]" by our unbelief, there is a point that His longsuffering comes to an end. We don't know when that will be, but Israel learned it was when they believed the ten spies instead of God.

Moving from the Physical to the Spiritual

So I swore in My wrath, "They shall not enter My rest" (Hebrews 3:11).

We would expect God to swear Israel could not enter the land, but He said they could not enter "My rest" (also in Hebrews 4:3). The Old Testament described the Promised Land as a place of rest: "Until the LORD has *given rest* to your brethren as to you, and they also *possess the land* which the LORD your God is giving them beyond the Jordan" (Deuteronomy 3:20).[4]

This is the first time the author of Hebrews uses the word "rest," looking beyond the physical rest in the Old Testament to the spiritual rest in the New Testament. Since the Promised Land prefigured a spiritual reality, it was always about more than a physical piece of land. John MacArthur said, "The application of

---

[4] See also Deuteronomy 12:9–10, Joshua 21:44, and 22:4.

this picture is to an individual's spiritual rest in the Lord, which has precedent in the Old Testament."[lxxvii] We see the precedent in verses offering God's people rest:

- *"Return to your rest, O my soul,* for the LORD has dealt bountifully with you" (Psalm 116:7).
- "To whom He said, *"This is the rest with which You may cause the weary to rest,"* and, "This is the refreshing"; yet they would not hear" (Isaiah 28:12).

An Important Warning

Beware, brethren, lest there be in any of you an evil
heart of unbelief in departing from the living God; but
exhort one another daily, while it is called "Today,"
lest any of you be hardened through the deceitfulness
of sin (Hebrews 3:12–13).

Israel "[departed] so far from [God]" they accused Him of murder: "Why has the LORD brought us to this land to fall by the sword, that our wives and children should become victims?" (Numbers 14:3).[5] The author wants to prevent his readers from doing the same; therefore, he says, "Beware," which is a word of warning, followed by "lest there be in any of you," to make it personal.

He exhorts each of us to "exhort one another." The Greek word for "exhort" is *parakaleo*, related to our word "parallel," because exhorting means coming alongside someone else.[lxxviii]

The phrase "deceitfulness of sin," reminds us sin lies. We need brothers and sisters in Christ who exhort us with the truth.

---

[5] See also Exodus 14:11–12 and 16:3.

176

Christians outside of fellowship open themselves up to many dangers, including deception.

The Need for Faith

> Therefore, since a promise remains of entering His rest, let us fear lest any of you seem to have come short of it. For indeed the gospel was preached to us as well as to them; but the word which they heard did not profit them, not being mixed with faith in those who heard it (Hebrews 4:1–2).

The word "Therefore," causes us to consider what was written previously—in this case, Israel's failure. The author transitions from talking about Israel to talking to his readers:

- Hebrews 3 contains the negative portion describing Israel's failure to enter
- Hebrews 4 contains the positive portion encouraging us (the readers) to enter

Since Israel didn't enter, "a promise remains of entering," but we should "fear" because of Israel's example. Knowing what happened to them is a warning to us. The words "come short" reveal how close they were; they came right up to the border of the Promised Land, but they were kept out.

Earlier God said Israel had "evil [hearts] of unbelief" (Hebrews 3:12). Typically, when we hear the word "evil," we think of actions, such as murder or rape, but not unbelief. Why describe their hearts as evil? Hebrews 3:9 says they "saw [God's] works forty years," and now the author says, "the gospel was preached...to them." They weren't ignorant. Their accountability was high. Second only to the generation in Jesus' day, is there another generation that had seen as much as the Israelites in the wilderness? They saw the plagues unleashed on Egypt and the Red Sea parting. They had every reason to believe, but they chose unbelief.

The words "to us as well," reveal another reason we should fear. We've heard the gospel too! We're not ignorant. Our accountability is high. We have every reason to believe, and failure to do so reveals that our hearts are evil.

We tend to think the Gospel is a New Testament invention, as though the Apostle Paul came up with it for the church. But the author of Hebrews said, "the gospel was preached to [Israel in the wilderness]." People have always been justified by grace alone, through faith alone, in Christ alone. The New Testament explains the gospel by quoting the Old Testament:

- Genesis 15:6 says, "[Abraham] believed in the LORD, and He accounted it to him for righteousness," and this is quoted in Romans 4:3, 9, 22, Galatians 3:6, and James 2:23.
- Habakkuk 2:4 says, "The just shall live by faith," and this is quoted in Romans 1:17, Galatians 3:11, and Hebrews 10:38.

We can go back further than Israel in the wilderness for more biblical evidence. Galatians 3:8 says God "preached the gospel to Abraham beforehand, saying, 'In you all the nations shall be blessed.'" This might not sound like a clear gospel presentation because it doesn't seem to mention Jesus, but He is the way "all the nations shall be blessed." If people believed this prophecy that God would bless the nations of the earth through one of Abraham's descendants, they were justified by faith. In the Old Testament, people looked forward in faith to Jesus coming, just as we look back in faith, believing He came.

We can go further back than Abraham to the moment sin entered the world. In Genesis 3:15, God told the serpent, "I will put enmity between you and the woman, and between your seed and her Seed; He shall bruise your head, and you shall bruise His heel." The words

"Seed," "He," and "His" are capitalized because they refer to Jesus. Genesis 3:15 is known as the *protoevangelium* or "first gospel" by many scholars as far back as the earliest church fathers, such as Justin Martyr in 160 AD and Irenaeus in 180 AD.[lxxix]

If people believed God would provide a Seed of the Woman who would crush the head of the serpent, then they were justified by faith. When sin was introduced into the world, the gospel was introduced as a way for man to be delivered from the consequence of sin, which is eternal punishment in hell.

The reason the gospel profited Adam, Eve, and Abraham is they believed, but it "did not profit [Israel because it was not] mixed (or combined) with faith." We're saved by grace *through faith*. Without grace, there's no faith. It's not just head knowledge of the gospel that profits. It's believing the gospel that profits.

Imagine people who know the Bible inside and out. It means nothing if they don't have faith. Jesus told the religious leaders:

> You do not have [the Father's] word abiding in you, because whom He sent, Him *you do not believe*. You search the Scriptures, for in them you think you have eternal life; and these are they which testify of Me. But you are not willing to come to Me that you may have life (John 5:38–40).

They didn't just read the Scriptures, they even "searched" it, but it profited them nothing because they didn't believe. On the other hand, the Thessalonians heard and believed:

> For this reason we also thank God without ceasing, because when you received the word of God which you heard from us, *you welcomed it not as the word of men, but as it is in truth, the word of God,* which also effectively works in you who believe" (1 Thessalonians 2:13).

Paul was blessed by the Thessalonians because they combined the gospel with faith. Now the author of Hebrews describes others who believe.

A Continual Rest

> For we *who have believed* do enter that rest, as He has said: "So I swore in My wrath, 'They shall not enter My rest,'" although the works were finished from the foundation of the world. For He has spoken in a certain place of the seventh day in this way: "And God rested on the seventh day from all His works" (Hebrews 4:3–4).

The corollary is: those who didn't believe couldn't enter, so those who do believe have entered. The failure of those unable to enter can't be attributed to the rest being incomplete or unavailable, because it's been "finished from the foundation of the world." God's rest existed well before Israel approached Canaan in 1400 BC. The words "And God rested on the seventh day from all His works," are from Genesis 2:2. This quote reveals the rest was established "from the foundation of the world," when He Himself rested. The rest was available then because even in Adam and Eve's day, it was possible to do the one thing necessary to enter the rest: believe.

Genesis 2:2 was written by Moses, but it's attributed to God ("For He has spoken"), giving more authority. This isn't what Moses says. This is what God has to say.[6]

---

[6] Hebrews 4:4 reads, "He has spoken in a certain place," versus "He has spoken in Genesis 2:2," because the chapter divisions weren't added until 1227, and the verses in 1551 as G.F Moore shows in *The Vulgate Chapters and Numbered Verses in the Hebrew Bible*, pages 73–78.

After each day of creation, Scripture says, "So the evening and the morning were the first/second/third/fourth/fifth/sixth day.[7] Then regarding the seventh day, Genesis 2:2–3 records:

> And on the seventh day God ended His work which He had done, and He rested on the seventh day from all His work which He had done. Then God blessed the seventh day and sanctified it, because in it He rested from all His work which God had created and made.

Although the evening is mentioned after the first six days, there's no mention of the evening after the seventh day because God's rest didn't come to an end. He didn't resume working the eighth day. He began a rest that continued indefinitely. Hebrews 4:1 says, it is "His rest," because it is associated with the rest He Himself entered; it is patterned after the rest He took. Three times God calls the rest "My rest," because it belongs to Him, can only be found in Him, and is given by Him.[8]

God rested and now offers that rest to us. Our rest can go on as continually for us as it went on for God. We can press into His rest and experience it every day, because "the gifts and the calling of God are irrevocable" (Romans 11:29) and "His mercy endures forever" (Psalm 136).[9]

Rest That Is Still Available

> And again in this place: "They shall not enter My rest." Since therefore it remains that some must enter it, and those to whom it was first preached did not

---

[7] Genesis 1:5, 8, 13, 19, 23, and 31.

[8] Hebrews 3:11, 4:3, and 4:5.

[9] See also Psalm 118:1–4, 29, and 2 Chronicles 20:21.

enter because of disobedience, again He designates a
certain day, saying in David, "Today," after such a
long time, as it has been said: "Today, if you will hear
His voice, do not harden your hearts" (Hebrews 4:5–
7).

Hebrews 4:5 quotes Psalm 95:11, which was also quoted in
Hebrews 3:11 and 4:3. Even though God's rest has been finished
since creation, the three-fold quote of Psalm 95:11 ("They shall not
enter My rest") emphasizes its emptiness. David wrote Psalm 95 in
approximately 1000 BC, which was four hundred years after Israel
failed to enter. The rest was still unfulfilled in David's day.

God doesn't make mistakes. He didn't create the rest so it would
sit empty. Thus, the words "therefore it remains that *some must enter.*"
God wants it occupied. Those in Moses' day and David's day didn't
enter, therefore, "again [God] designates a certain day." Since
nobody entered, it's still available.

God's Rest Is Not about a Physical Location

David wrote Psalm 95, which is to say God spoke "in David," when
he was in the Promised Land. By that time, Israel had been in the
land for four hundred years. If David and Israel's presence in the
land meant it was occupied, it would not make sense for God to say
"some must enter it" centuries later. The physical land couldn't
provide the spiritual rest. Those who didn't believe experienced the
land, but not the rest.

Ronald Sauer writes, "Divine rest, then, is more than life in
Canaan; that literal rest is but a type of its spiritual counterpart."[lxxx]
Since the rest is spiritual instead of physical, it is available regardless
of physical location or circumstances:

- If we believe, we can experience God's rest, wherever we are
  and regardless of what's going on in our lives.

- If we don't believe, we can't experience God's rest, no matter where we are and regardless of what's going on in our lives.

The author used the word "today" in Hebrews 3:7, 13, 15, and again in 4:7. How much more could he emphasize urgency and the present to his readers? Although we are justified in a moment, once-for-all-time, there's a need to daily enter God's promised rest. We can wake up each morning and say, "I believe God. I trust Him. Today I will enter His rest." We are left with a now and not yet reality—in this life we enjoy God's rest, but we look forward to heaven, where we will be able to experience the true and greater reality of eternal rest.

The words "Do not harden your hearts" are also repeated in Hebrews 4:7 for the fourth and final time, because there's no guarantee the rest will be available tomorrow. Just as Israel missed the physical rest (the Promised Land) in Moses' day, we can miss the spiritual rest in our day.

Hebrews 3:19 says, "So we see that they could not enter in because of unbelief." Just as Israel was prevented from entering because of unbelieving hearts, we can also be prevented from entering because of unbelieving hearts.

Resting God's way means resting both physically and spiritually. For some people, they might rest physically, but they neglect the spiritual rest they need. They nourish their bodies, but not their souls. We must find the right balance, not just between work and rest, but between physical rest and spiritual rest. In the following chapter, we'll consider the Sabbath and why we can rest—because of the finished work of Christ.

Chapter Seventeen

The Sabbath and Spiritual Rest

For if Joshua had given them rest, God would not
have spoken of another day later on. So then, there
remains a Sabbath rest for the people of God, for
whoever has entered God's rest has also rested from
his works as God did from his (Hebrews 4:8–10
ESV).

A right is a freedom given to people and protected by a
government's laws. For example, American citizens have the
right to express themselves, worship as they wish, and vote in
elections for public officials.

A privilege is an opportunity or advantage given to people who
meet certain conditions. For example, driving is a privilege for
people who have reached an age, passed a test, and agreed to obey
the rules of the road.

The author of Hebrews wrote to his readers about a privilege
they could be given, and that's entering "a Sabbath rest." The
condition they had to meet is contained in the words "for the people
of God." If the readers became God's people, they could experience
His rest.

Since Gentiles were coming into the church, the Hebrew readers felt as though they were losing their status. The author of Hebrews explains that the only way they could remain the "people of God" was not by descending from Abraham, but by believing:

- Unbelieving Jews would lose their privileged status even if they were in the Promised Land and even if they observed the Sabbath.
- Believing Gentiles became the people of God even if they weren't in the Promised Land and even if they didn't observe the Sabbath.

The words, "there remains" reveal the rest is available now, as opposed to only being available in the future when we get to heaven. The Greek word for "rest" in the previous verses is *katapausis,*[lxxxi] but the word for "Sabbath rest" in Hebrews 4:9 is *sabbatismos,*[lxxxii] and this is the only place it occurs in Scripture. The words "there remains a Sabbath rest for the people of God" are similar to Hebrews 4:1 "Therefore, since a promise remains of entering His rest," but whereas the Promised Land was in view earlier, now the Sabbath is in view. Just as the Promised Land prefigured God's rest, so too does the Sabbath.

The point the author of Hebrews is making is spiritual rather than physical; he is not primarily referring to physically resting from work. Instead, he is referring to spiritually resting from working for salvation. The Sabbath rest also looks back to creation when "[God] rested from His works." He rested on the seventh day because His work was finished, and we can rest because the work for our salvation is finished. Just as God didn't resume working again on the eighth day, we don't resume working for our salvation on a later day. We enter God's rest by trusting what Jesus has already and fully accomplished on our behalf.

Notice it doesn't say those who have entered will cease from their works. It says they "[have already] ceased from [their] works as God did from His." We don't enter the rest and then cease working for salvation. We have entered the rest because we have ceased working for salvation.

Resting in Jesus' Finished Work

The priests might have been the hardest workers in the Old Testament. Jesus said, "On the Sabbath the priests in the temple profane the Sabbath, and are blameless" (Matthew 12:5). They didn't even get to rest on the Sabbath! The tabernacle and temple had many furnishings, but none for resting because the priests' work was never done:

> Every priest stands ministering daily and offering
> repeatedly the same sacrifices, which can never take
> away sins. But this Man, after He had offered one
> sacrifice for sins forever, sat down at the right hand of
> God (Hebrews 10:11–12).

Priests had to continually offer sacrifices because none of them could "take away sins." This meant they did not experience permanent rest. In contrast, Jesus is "the Lamb of God *who takes away the sin of the world*" (John 1:29). As our High Priest, He "sat down" because His work was done. Jesus rested, and He offers that rest to us:

> Come to Me, all you who labor and are heavy laden,
> and *I will give you rest*. Take My yoke upon you and
> learn from Me, for I am gentle and lowly in heart, and
> *you will find rest for your souls*. For My yoke is easy and
> My burden is light (Matthew 11:28–30).

Jesus offers rest to "all who labor and are heavy laden," which is how anyone must feel trying to keep the Mosaic Law to be saved.

Peter said it is "a yoke on the neck [that] neither our fathers nor we were able to bear" (Acts 15:10) and Paul said it is a "yoke of bondage" (Galatians 5:1). But Jesus said His yoke is "easy," and His "burden is light."

We can rest in the salvation Jesus provides. We don't have to wonder if we've done enough because it's not about what we do. It's about what Jesus has done. It's not based on our work, but on Christ's work on our behalf. It's not about our unrighteousness. It's about Jesus' righteousness imputed to our account. I rest because Jesus, my Advocate, sat down at the right hand of His Father in glory.

Work Hard to Rest?

> Let us therefore be diligent to enter that rest, lest anyone fall according to the same example of disobedience (Hebrews 4:11).

By repeating the word "today" five times in the previous verses, the focus was on the urgency of entering.[1] Now the words "let us therefore be diligent" focus on the effort needed to enter. The word "us" shows the author included himself. He knew he needed to do everything he told his readers to do! Everyone—even the authors of Scripture—must be diligent to enter God's rest! This brings us full circle. We've spoken of the importance of diligence regarding the physical, and now we see the importance of diligence regarding the spiritual.

There is a paradox. We enter by believing, but belief doesn't require effort. It seems inconsistent to say we must work hard (be diligent) while also saying we must rest. How can this be resolved? John 6:28–29 records:

---

[1] In Hebrews 3:7, 3:13, 3:15, and twice in 4:7.

> They said to [Jesus], "What shall we do, that we may
> *work the works of God?*"
> Jesus answered and said to them, "This is the work of
> God, that you *believe in Him* whom He sent."

When we think of work, we don't think of believing. We think of doing something. Jesus used the word "work" ironically. The people were convinced they should work to earn God's favor. Jesus said they must abandon confidence in their efforts and trust wholly in Him and the work He would do. Their "work" is to believe that their work will never save them; only Christ's finished work can do so. That is what true saving faith is, not a thing we do that prompts God to be gracious to us. Faith is the God-given gift, the instrument by which we lay hold of Christ and all his merits.

The Greek word for work is *ergon,* and it means, "to undertake or become occupied with an enterprise."[lxxxiii] As Christians, our enterprise is believing and being occupied with Jesus. It is our belief that pleases God. As the author of Hebrews later says, "Without faith it is impossible to please Him, for he who comes to God must believe that He is" (Hebrews 11:6). Believing is the work God wants, and when we believe, we can spiritually rest, because we need no longer work.

The Promised Land and the Sabbath foreshadowed our spiritual rest in Christ. To appreciate this beautiful truth, we must understand one of the purposes of the Old Testament.

The Old Testament Is about Jesus

When Philip recognized Jesus as the Messiah, he told Nathaniel, "We have found Him of whom Moses in the law, and also the Prophets, wrote—Jesus of Nazareth, the son of Joseph" (John 1:45). The "Law and the Prophets" was a title for the Old Testament before the New Testament was written (Matthew 7:12, Acts 13:15,

Romans 3:12). Philip understood the Old Testament was about Jesus.

Jesus also said the Old Testament is about Him:

- "Beginning at Moses and all the Prophets, [Jesus] expounded to them in all the Scriptures the things concerning Himself" (Luke 24:27).
- "[Jesus] said, 'All things must be fulfilled which were written in the Law of Moses and the Prophets and the Psalms concerning Me'" (Luke 24:44).
- "[Jesus said,] 'Behold, I have come—in the volume of the book it is written of Me'" (Hebrews 10:7).

How is the Old Testament about Jesus? He is primarily revealed in two ways. First, there are prophecies of Him. For example:

- Genesis 49:10 prophesied He would be from the tribe of Judah.
- Second Samuel 7:12–13 prophesied He would receive King David's throne.
- Isaiah 50:6 prophesied He would be spat upon and beaten.
- Isaiah 53:7 prophesied He would be silent in the face of accusations.
- Hosea 11:1 prophesied He would spend a season in Egypt.
- Zechariah 9:9 prophesied He would ride into Jerusalem on a donkey.

And the list goes on. And on. And on. Jesus fulfilled around 350 prophecies in His first coming.[lxxxiv]

The second way the Old Testament reveals Jesus is through types or shadows:

- Hebrews 10:1 says, "The law [was only] *a shadow of the good things to come* instead of the true form of these realities" (ESV).

- Colossians 2:16–17 says a "festival or a new moon or sabbaths [are] *a shadow of things to come*, but the substance is of Christ."

"Shadows" are a fitting way to describe the types of Christ in the Old Testament because shadows provide an idea of what something looks like without completely revealing the object. The Old Testament does this with Christ. A shadow is evidence that something or someone is casting the shadow; in this case, Christ is the Someone. Finally, nobody looks at a shadow and believes it is the real thing. Nobody sees the shadow of a tree or car and thinks it's a tree or car, because shadows have no substance; they are not the reality. According to Colossians 2:17, Jesus is the substance, and according to Hebrews 10:1, He is the reality.

The New Testament identifies many types and shadows of Christ in the Old Testament. For example:

- John 3:14 compares Jesus with the Bronze Serpent: "As Moses lifted up the serpent in the wilderness, even so must the Son of Man be lifted up."
- John 6:32–33 compares Jesus with the manna: "Moses did not give you the bread from heaven, but My Father gives you the true bread from heaven. For the bread of God is He who comes down from heaven and gives life to the world."
- Romans 5:14 compares Jesus with Adam: "Adam is a type of Him who was to come."
- First Corinthians 5:7 compares Jesus with the Passover Lamb: "For indeed Christ, our Passover, was sacrificed for us."
- First Corinthians 10:4 compares Jesus with the rock that accompanied Israel in the wilderness: "[Israel] drank of that spiritual Rock that followed them, and that Rock was Christ."

- Hebrews 10:20 compares Jesus' body with the veil in the temple that when "torn" on the cross revealed the access believers have to the Father: "[We have] a new and living way [to God] which [Jesus] consecrated for us, through the veil, [which] is, His flesh."

Miracles in the Old Testament prefigured some miracles Jesus would perform in a greater way:

- God took Elijah up to heaven in a whirlwind (2 Kings 2:11), but Jesus ascended to heaven on His own (Acts 1:9).
- Elisha fed one hundred men with twenty loaves (2 Kings 4:42–44), but Jesus fed 5,000 and 4,000 men with five and seven loaves (Matthew 14:13–21 and 15:32–39).
- Elisha cleansed one man of leprosy (2 Kings 5:1–14), but Jesus cleansed ten men (Luke 17:11–19).
- Elisha knew what Gehazi had done (2 Kings 5:26), but Jesus knows what all men have done (John 2:24).
- Elisha's death gave one person temporary life (2 Kings 13:21), but Jesus' death gives many people eternal life (Romans 5:18).

Certain practices looked forward to Christ. Each sacrifice for sin looked forward to Jesus—the perfect Sacrifice for sins. Circumcision has its fulfillment in Christ because He helps us put off our sinful flesh: "In [Christ] you were circumcised…without hands by putting off…the flesh, by the circumcision of Christ" (Colossians 2:11).

What is the purpose of all the prophecies and shadows? To lead people to Christ! Jesus said, "All the prophets and the law prophesied until John" (Matthew 11:13). Jesus was veiled throughout the Old Testament in the types and shadows, but when John the Baptist arrived as Jesus' forerunner, He was no longer veiled. John pointed at Him and said, "Behold! The Lamb of God who takes away the sin of the world!" (John 1:29).

When we come to Jesus, He becomes the reality of all the types and shadows, including the Promised Land and the Sabbath. Just as belief would've allowed Israel to enter the Promised Land, belief allows us to enter the rest found in Jesus: "We who have believed do enter that rest" (Hebrews 4:3). When we enter the spiritual rest found in Jesus, we don't enjoy it for one day like the people did with the Sabbath in the Old Testament. We enjoy it every day.

Are You in the Wilderness, or Have you Entered the Rest?

The Old Testament typology found in Joshua, Egypt, and Moses is crucial to understand. Then we can examine ourselves and see where we are in our spiritual journeys.

Joshua Is a Type of Jesus

In Hebrews 4:8, the author said, "For if Joshua had given them rest, then He would not afterward have spoken of another day." Joshua and Jesus have the same name, but Jesus is Greek, and Joshua is Hebrew. They both mean, "Jehovah is salvation":

- Joshua led God's people in the Old Testament into the physical rest (Promised Land).
- Jesus leads God's people in the New Testament into the spiritual rest.

Jesus is better than Joshua because He leads people into the better rest.

Egypt Is a Type of the World

Joseph invited his brothers and their families into Egypt; seventy people total (Exodus 1:5). They "were fruitful and increased abundantly...and the land was filled with them" (Exodus 1:7).

Exodus 12:37 says Moses delivered six hundred thousand men from Egypt, which means there were probably around two-to-three million people total. Egypt served as a womb for Israel to grow from seventy people to millions of people. Israel's journey parallels ours:

- Israel was born in Egypt like we're born into the world.
- Israel was delivered from Egypt like we're delivered from the world.
- Israel struggled with wanting to return to Egypt (Exodus 14:3, 16:3, 17:3, Numbers 14:3, 20:5), like we struggle with wanting to return to the world.
- Israel turned to Egypt for help instead of turning to God (2 Kings 18:21, Isaiah 36:6, Ezekiel 17:15) as we turn to the world for help instead of turning to God.
- God brought Israel out of Egypt into the Promised Land, like He brings us out of the world into His rest.

Moses Is a Type of the Law
The Law was given to Moses, which is why it's known as "The Law of Moses" and "The Mosaic Law." Moses delivered Israel from Egypt the way the Law delivers us from the world: "By the law is the knowledge of sin" (Romans 3:20). The Law convicts us of sin, we repent and turn from the world to Jesus.

Consider how this illustrates Galatians 3:23–25:

- As Israel was under Moses we were under the law: "We were kept under guard by the law (Galatians 3:23).
- As Israel was then under Joshua, we were then under Christ: "Therefore the law was our tutor to bring us to Christ, that we might be justified by faith" (Galatians 3:24).
- As Israel was no longer under Moses when they were under Joshua, we are no longer under the law when we are under

Jesus: "But after faith has come, we are no longer under a tutor" (Galatians 3:25).

Delivered from Egypt, but Dying in the Wilderness

Israel made it out of Egypt because they were redeemed at Passover. God wanted them to enter the Promised Land versus spend their lives wandering in the wilderness. Two groups developed. The first group entered under Joshua and experienced rest. The second group remained under Moses, and didn't experience rest.

Tragically, the Hebrew readers were in danger of spiritually being part of the second group:

- Many of the Israelites only made it partway in their journeys out of Egypt, and the author of Hebrews wrote to readers who only made it partway in their journeys out of the world.
- The Israelites died in the wilderness under Moses, and the Hebrew readers were in danger of dying in the spiritual wilderness under the Law (Moses).
- The Israelites didn't make it into the Promised Land under Joshua, and the Hebrew readers were in danger of not making it into the spiritual Promised Land, or rest, under Jesus (Joshua).

Although, the danger isn't only for the Hebrew readers in the first century. As believers, we find ourselves in one of the above groups. As Israel was delivered from Egypt by Passover, we're delivered from the world by "Christ, our Passover" (1 Corinthians 5:7). After God delivers us from the world, our Egypt, He doesn't want us spending our lives wandering in the wilderness. He wants us to enter the Promised Land and experience rest.

Just as Moses could only take Israel so far, the Law can only take us so far. Just as Israel couldn't enter under Moses, we can't enter under the Law. Why? Because there's no rest under the Law. Israel had to be under Joshua like we must be under Jesus. Just as Israel turned back and forfeited the Promised Land, if we turn back from Jesus, we forfeit the spiritual rest He offers.

Following the True and Greater Moses and Joshua

Hebrews 3:3 says Jesus "has been counted worthy of more glory than Moses," and Hebrews 4:8 says, "Joshua [has not] given them rest." Jesus is greater than Moses and Joshua. If Israel was expected to follow Moses and Joshua, how much more are we expected to follow Jesus?

If we don't follow Jesus, we're wandering like Israel. Their wilderness was physical and ours is spiritual, but we can perish in ours as much as they perished in theirs. The solution is to press on "since therefore it remains that some must enter it" (Hebrews 4:6). God didn't create the spiritual rest to sit empty. He wants it occupied for our blessing and His worship: "That we who first trusted in Christ should be to the praise of His glory" (Ephesians 1:12, 14). As we'll discuss in the next chapter, resting God's way means trusting Jesus' finished work on the cross, and experiencing all the accompanying riches.

Chapter Eighteen

Are You Working and Resting God's Way?

One month after high school graduation, Joni Eareckson Tada broke her neck when diving off a raft in the shallows of the Chesapeake Bay. She attended multiple healing services and obeyed verses that she thought would qualify her for physical restoration, such as confessing sins and having elders pray over her and anoint her with oil. Yet her arms and legs remained unresponsive. She became critical of Jesus, saying, "What kind of Savior? What kind of rescuer, what kind of healer, what kind of deliverer would refuse the prayer of a paralytic?"[lxxxv]

A pivotal moment in Joni's life occurred when she reread the account with the paralyzed man lowered through the roof by his friends. In Luke 5:20, Jesus said, "Man, your sins are forgiven you." The religious leaders accused Him of blasphemy because only God can forgive sins. Jesus responded:

> "Why are you reasoning in your hearts? Which is easier, to say, 'Your sins are forgiven you,' or to say, 'Rise up and walk'? But that you may know that the Son of Man has power on earth to forgive sins"—He said to the man who was paralyzed, "I say to you,

arise, take up your bed, and go to your house" (Luke 5:22–24).

The account convinced Tada that Jesus' greatest desire for us is spiritual versus physical—rescuing us from sin, versus rescuing us from physical suffering.[lxxxvi] If this is the case, then how do we explain Jesus performing so many physical healings? What application do these accounts have for us?

Most of what Jesus did physically is a picture of what He wants to do for us spiritually. Failure to understand this has led to countless theological errors. In Matthew 13:14, Jesus said, "Hearing you will hear and shall not understand, and seeing you will see and not perceive." People in Jesus' day heard and saw physically, but not spiritually. When Jesus healed physical blindness and deafness, the application isn't that Jesus wants to heal every blind and deaf person. Instead, it reveals His desire to help us see and hear spiritually.

When Jesus healed the paralytic, the application isn't that He wants to heal every paralyzed person, as evidenced by Joni's life. Instead, He wants to heal our spiritual lameness: "Therefore we were buried with Him through baptism into death, that just as Christ was raised from the dead by the glory of the Father, even so we also *should walk in newness of life*" (Romans 6:4).

There were problems when people interpreted physically what He meant spiritually:

- Jesus told Nicodemus, "Unless one is born again, he cannot see the kingdom of God." Nicodemus responded, "How can a man be born when he is old? Can he enter a second time into his mother's womb and be born?" (John 3:3–4). Jesus was speaking of spiritual birth, but Nicodemus thought He was speaking of a second physical birth.
- Jesus told the woman at the well, "If you knew the gift of God, and who it is who says to you, 'Give Me a drink,' you would have asked Him, and He would have given you living

water." The woman said to Him, "Sir, You have nothing to draw with, and the well is deep. Where then do You get that living water? Are You greater than our father Jacob, who gave us the well, and drank from it himself, as well as his sons and his livestock?" (John 4:10–12). Jesus was speaking of spiritual water, but she thought He was referring to the physical water in the well.

- Jesus told the crowds that followed Him, "I am the living bread which came down from heaven. If anyone eats of this bread, he will live forever; and the bread that I shall give is My flesh, which I shall give for the life of the world.' The Jews, therefore, quarreled among themselves, saying, 'How can this Man give us His flesh to eat?'" (John 6:51–52). Jesus was speaking spiritually of Himself as the true bread from heaven, but they thought He was promoting cannibalism.

After Jesus fed the five thousand, thousands more began following Him. But they had missed the spiritual significance of what He had done. They saw the miracle physically, but they didn't understand it spiritually; therefore, they were following Jesus, not because they wanted spiritual food, Jesus Himself, but because they wanted more physical food. Jesus said to them, "Most assuredly, I say to you, you seek Me, not because you saw the signs, but because you ate of the loaves and were filled" (John 6:26).

It looks like Jesus is saying they didn't see the miracle He performed, but of course they did; that's why they were following Him. When Jesus said they did not see the signs, He meant they saw His miracles physically, but not spiritually. Jesus' miracles are called "signs" because they point to something spiritual. Jesus wanted the crowds following Him to hunger spiritually, but they only hungered physically because they didn't understand His miracles.

Jesus Satisfies Spiritually

Jesus was forced to spell out the spiritual truth in each instance. He told Nicodemus, "Most assuredly, I say to you, unless one is born of water and the Spirit, he cannot enter the kingdom of God" (John 3:5). In other words, "No, Nicodemus, I'm not talking about physical birth into the world; I'm talking about spiritual birth into My kingdom."

He told the crowds following Him, "I am the bread of life. He who comes to Me shall *never hunger*" (John 6:35). Similarly, He told the woman at the well, "Whoever drinks of this water will thirst again, but whoever drinks of the water that I shall give him will *never thirst*." (John 4:13–14). Jesus didn't mean that we would never hunger or thirst again physically, but He did mean that He alone would satisfy our spiritual hunger and thirst. In Luke 6:21, Jesus said, "Blessed are you who hunger now, for you shall be satisfied." Not physically, but spiritually. After Jesus fed the five thousand, it says, "And they all ate and were satisfied" (Luke 9:17 ESV). This physically pictured the spiritual reality.

When I became a Christian in my early twenties, God gave me new desires. In other words, I hungered and thirsted in different ways—I wanted to get married, have children, become a pastor, and the list could go on. Although, I can sincerely say I never hungered or thirsted again spiritually. I was satisfied. I didn't wonder what other religions offered. I didn't question whether other sacred texts contained truth I was missing. I am not sharing this testimony remotely as any credit to myself. I say it as a credit to Christ's ability to satisfy us spiritually.

Jesus Provides Spiritual Peace

When the disciples were caught in a storm that they thought would drown them, they woke Jesus. Mark 4:39 says, "Then He arose and rebuked the wind, and said to the sea, 'Peace, be still!' And the wind ceased and *there was a great calm.*" Jesus took a very tumultuous situation and provided great peace. The application from this miracle is not that Jesus calms every physical storm that we encounter. Instead, it reveals the spiritual calm Jesus provides in all circumstances.

As a pastor, I would love to be able to tell people, "If you're experiencing a storm, call out to the Lord, and He'll calm it for you as He did for the disciples." The problem, though, is this might not be true. There are storms God allows to rage throughout our lives:

- Diseases aren't always cured
- Broken relationships aren't always fixed
- Financial situations don't always improve

Since these storms aren't calmed, then what does Jesus do for us? He might not bring peace to the storms that rage outside us, but He can bring peace to the storms that rage inside us. He brings "a great calm" to our tumultuous hearts. The storms around us don't always stop, but the storms inside us can be stilled. The physical rest Jesus brought in the middle of that sea two thousand years ago pictures the spiritual rest He can bring in the middle of the storms we face.

Isaiah 26:3 does not say, "You will keep him in perfect peace, whose life is free from storms and trials." Instead, it says, "You will keep him in perfect peace, whose mind is stayed on You, because he trusts in You." When the disciples were terrified, they should've rested because Jesus was in the boat with them. If we're Christians, we can have peace and rest through storms because we know Jesus is in the boat with us, and He's in control.

Romans 5:1 says, "Having been justified by faith, *we have peace with God* through our Lord Jesus Christ." After we have "peace with

God" we can have the "peace of God" described in Philippians 4:6–7:

> Be anxious for nothing, but in everything by prayer
> and supplication, with thanksgiving, let your requests
> be made known to God; and *the peace of God*, which
> surpasses all understanding, will guard your hearts and
> minds through Christ Jesus.

It doesn't say, "peace that surpasses understanding, because your storm ceases." Instead, it's peace we can have in our "hearts and minds" because of our relationships with Jesus. It "surpasses all understanding" in that we might not even understand why we're at peace and rest. The circumstances in our lives fill us with turmoil and anxiety, but Jesus provides a spiritual calm in our hearts.

Restoring Rest

Prior to The Fall, Adam and Eve were at rest in its original and fullest sense. They relied on God for everything. They had no anxiety, pain, frustration, needs, or heartache:

- They didn't struggle with God's forgiveness because they had no sin.
- They didn't doubt God's love because they had no reason to believe He might not love them.
- They didn't need God's consolation because they were never grieved.
- They didn't need His encouragement because they were never discouraged.

They only needed His fellowship, which they had. They were at rest. When The Fall took place, Adam and Eve's rest was gone. Sin introduced anxiety, stress, and worry, but through Christ, peace and rest can be restored.

Resting in Christ's Victory over Death

Hebrews 2:15 says Jesus "[releases] those who through *fear of death* were all their lifetime subject to bondage." This doesn't say people are in bondage to death, although that's true. This says people are in bondage to the fear of death! Jesus frees us from that bondage:

> So when this corruptible has put on incorruption, and this mortal has put on immortality, then shall be brought to pass the saying that is written: "Death is swallowed up in victory. O Death, where is your sting? O Hades, where is your victory?" The sting of Death is sin, and the strength of sin is the law. But thanks be to God, who gives us the victory through our Lord Jesus Christ (1 Corinthians 15:54–57).

Death is capitalized to personify it as an enemy Jesus defeats: "The last enemy that will be destroyed is Death" (1 Corinthians 15:26). To emphasize how clearly Death is defeated, Revelation 20:14 says, "Death [is] cast into the lake of fire." God sends Death to hell! So, we can be confident and rest in Jesus' victory over it. First John 5:13 says, "These things I have written to you who believe in the name of the Son of God, that *you may know that you have eternal life*" (1 John 5:13). How much rest is there for people who spent their lives fearing Death to come to know a future heavenly home awaits them?

Resting in Deliverance from the Power of Sin

Romans 6:11 commands us to, "reckon [ourselves] dead indeed to sin, but alive to God in Christ Jesus our Lord." We're freed from life-dominating sins. Imagine the rest for people who previously spent their lives running from addiction to addiction and broken relationship to broken relationship.

Resting in Forgiveness

Some people spend years struggling with guilt from sins they committed. Romans 8:1 says, "There is therefore now no condemnation to those who are in Christ Jesus." We're freed from shame. Consider the rest for people who learn that Jesus took the punishment their sins deserve. Since Jesus paid for those sins, they no longer need to grieve over them.

Jesus Is Our Inheritance

Let's tie this back to our discussion of the Promised Land. Israel was to look beyond the land physically to see God as their portion spiritually:

- "*The LORD is my portion*," says my soul, "Therefore I hope in Him" (Lamentations 3:24).
- "I cried out to You, O LORD: I said, 'You are my refuge, *My portion* in the land of the living'" (Psalm 142:5).

The Promised Land was Israel's inheritance (or portion) in the Old Testament, and it foreshadowed Jesus as our inheritance in the New Testament. As Israel was to possess all the land, we seek to possess all that we have in Christ. After Joshua and the nation experienced many victories, God said to him, "You are old, advanced in years, and *there remains very much land yet to be possessed*" (Joshua 13:1). Although Israel owned all the land, they still had more of it to possess. Ephesians 1:3 says the Father has "blessed us with *every spiritual blessing* in the heavenly places in Christ." Although we own all the spiritual blessings, we always have more of Christ to possess.

We might expect God to say these words to Joshua when he was young, and the nation had just entered the land. Instead, God said this to him toward the end of his life after they'd already possessed a considerable portion. It would've been easy for Joshua to look at all he had done and want to relax, but God wanted him to press on. The same is true for us. We rest in the finished work of Christ, accomplished and applied to our lives, but God wants us to press on.

No matter how close we are to finishing the race, we always have more to do. If anyone looked like he reached the goal and could rest, it's the apostle Paul. But in Philippians 3:12–14, he said:

> Not that I have already [obtained], or am already perfected; but *I press on*, that I may lay hold of that for which Christ Jesus has also laid hold of me. Brethren, I do not count myself to have apprehended; but one thing I do, forgetting those things which are behind and *reaching forward* to those things which are ahead, I *press toward* the goal for the prize of the upward call of God in Christ Jesus.

Even at the end of Paul's life, he wanted to keep advancing because, as God told Joshua, there was more. We should be like Paul and press on toward our heavenly goal. We can spend our lives without ever possessing all the inheritance we have in Christ, because if we keep pursuing Him, He keeps offering us more:

- More to do for the Lord
- More to know about the Lord
- More to grow in our relationships with the Lord

What If You Were a Levite?

Instead of receiving a physical inheritance in the land, one of the tribes received a spiritual inheritance. Joshua 13:33 says, "To the tribe of Levi Moses had *given no inheritance; the LORD God of Israel was their inheritance*, as He had said to them." The Levites provide an Old Testament glimpse of the New Testament reality for the church.

The situation they experienced—having something spiritual versus physical—is like the true believer's experience today. We don't receive a physical inheritance. Our inheritance is spiritual. Just as the Levites enjoyed the Lord Himself as their inheritance, we enjoy and rest in the Lord as our inheritance.

Consider for a moment that you're a Levite, and you don't receive a physical inheritance in the land even though all the other tribes do. You receive the news that the Lord Himself is your inheritance. Do you feel slighted? Is the Lord enough for you? Are you content with the spiritual, or do you wish you had something physical instead? You can answer by considering whether you're satisfied with Christ.

Working and Resting God's Way

It is said that man has three basic needs in life: love, purpose, and significance. Many times, we try to find purpose in work itself. Solomon detailed his search for meaning in a variety of projects and activities:

> I made my works great, I built myself houses, and
> planted myself vineyards. I made myself gardens and
> orchards, and I planted all kinds of fruit trees in them.
> I made myself water pools from which to water the
> growing trees of the grove...I had greater possessions
> of herds and flocks than all who were in Jerusalem
> before me (Ecclesiastes 2:4–7).

Even though the work brought some degree of satisfaction, he concluded:

> For my heart rejoiced in all my labor; and this was my
> reward from all my labor. Then I looked on all the
> works that my hands had done and on the labor in
> which I had toiled; and *indeed all was vanity and grasping
> for the wind. There was no profit under the sun* (Ecclesiastes
> 2:10–11).

Solomon's work was vain because he engaged in it apart from his Creator. Work is of no value except when it is done for God.

The people who lived in the land of Shinar after the Flood are another example of what to avoid. They constructed the Tower of Babel, which was no small feat of work in the ancient world. They said, "Come, let us build ourselves a city, and a tower whose top is in the heavens; *let us make a name for ourselves*, lest we be scattered abroad over the face of the whole earth" (Genesis 11:4). Their pride and self-focus are revealed through the words "make a name for [themselves]." They wanted to work, but for their glory.

As long as we are on this side of heaven "under the sun," our attitude toward work should mirror that of our Lord: "My food is to do the will of Him who sent Me, and to *finish His work*" (John 4:34). It should be our desire as well to finish the work—physical and spiritual—God has for us for His glory. As God commands, "Whatever you do in word or deed, *do all in the name of the Lord Jesus*" (Colossians 3:17). Working God's way means working "in the name of the Lord Jesus," so He can be exalted.

First Corinthians 10:31 commands, "Whatever you do, *do all to the glory of God.*" We can't glory in ourselves, because we are only doing what God laid out for us: "We are His workmanship, created in Christ Jesus for good works, *which God prepared beforehand* that we should walk in them" (Ephesians 2:10). Working God's way means working for His glory.

Paradoxically, we can rest even when working, because our work was "prepared beforehand." We're no longer anxiously flailing about trying to earn God's favor. We're resting in Christ, and, thus, joyfully working in His vineyard. Our spiritual rest and sanctified labor are connected in that one enables the other. Confidence in God's sovereignty frees us from worry because we know God is in control. We're liberated from striving, manipulating, and straining: "Rest in the LORD, and wait patiently for Him" (Psalm 37:7).

Resting God's way means trusting God will bring about the best end.

Spiritually, we rest because the work for our salvation is accomplished. On the cross, Jesus said, "It is finished" (John 19:30). His work was done, so He "sat down at the right hand of God" (Mark 16:19). We don't have to wonder if we've done enough because it's not about what we do. It's about what Jesus has done. It's not based on our work, but on Christ's finished work for us. Resting God's way means resting in the salvation Jesus provided, and that frees us to do the work He has prepared for us.

About the Author

Scott is the senior pastor of Woodland
Christian Church in Woodland,
Washington, and a conference speaker. He
and his wife, Katie, grew up together in
northern California, and God has blessed
them with eight children.

You can contact Pastor Scott or learn
more about him at the following:

- Email: scott@scottlapierre.org
- Website: www.scottlapierre.org
- Facebook: @ScottLaPierreAuthor
- YouTube: @ScottLaPierre
- Twitter: @PastorWCC
- Instagram: @PastorWCC

Receive a Free Copy of One of Scott's Books

Download your free copy of *Seven Biblical
Insights for Healthy, Joyful, Christ-Centered Marriages:
And Accompanying Discussion Questions to Apply
Them.* Each insight is followed by discussion
questions you should answer with your spouse
(or boyfriend, girlfriend, or fiancé).
www.scottlapierre.org/subscribe/

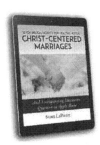

Would You Like to Invite Pastor Scott to Speak at Your Event?

You can expect:

- Professionally prepared and delivered messages
- Handouts with lessons and discussion questions
- Copies of Pastor Scott's books to offer as gifts to increase registrations (if you desire)
- Prompt replies to communication
- Advertising of your event on Pastor Scott's social media

Schedule for Conferences—Typically, there are one or two sessions on Friday evening and three or four sessions on Saturday, but there is flexibility: conferences can be spread over three days or kept to one day, and Q&A sessions can be added.

Outreach—Consider viewing the conference as an outreach to share Christ with your community. Pastor Scott can run a Facebook ad and/or set up a Facebook event page for those in the church to share with others.

For more information, including sample messages and endorsements, please visit:

www.scottlapierre.org/conferences-and-speaking.

Also Available from Scott LaPierre

Be sure to check out the *Work and Rest God's Way Family Guide*

The *Family Guide* is the perfect complement to *Work and Rest God's Way*!

Christian family books are hard to find. If you're looking for Christian workbooks for adults or a Christian workbook for kids, look no further! Inside you will find questions and activities that make this the family workbook parents and kids can enjoy working through together.

The discipline to work can be challenging for all of us, but motivating children to work is especially difficult. As a father of eight, Pastor Scott knows what is needed. Let him help you teach your children what the Bible says about work. The Family Guide is the culmination of what has been successful for him and his wife, Katie.

Whether you're a man or woman, young or old, parent or child, married or single, this guide will enable you to enjoy both work and rest as God intended. Each question and activity will help you and your family discover joy and purpose in all you do.

Marriage God's Way: A Biblical Recipe for Healthy, Joyful, Christ-Centered Relationships

Nearly everything in life comes with instructions, from the cell phones we use to the automobiles we drive. Yet when it comes to marriage, many people struggle without proper guidance. Pastor  Scott presents the needed biblical instructions combined with:

- Personal stories and application to daily life
- Explanations of the roles and responsibilities God has given husbands and wives
- Answers to common questions about godly love and how to show it, headship and submission, intimacy, and establishing an indestructible foundation for your relationship

Endorsed by well-known ministry leaders:

- "The reader will be richly rewarded."
  Tedd Tripp—Best-selling author of *Shepherding a Child's Heart*
- "This is what every marriage needs!"
  Scott Brown—Founder of The National Center for Family-Integrated Churches and author of *A Theology of the Family*

Enduring Trials God's Way: A Biblical Recipe for Finding Joy in Suffering

Trials are part of life on this side of heaven, and God wants to use them for your good! Learn scriptural principles that give you the encouragement you need when suffering. Every chapter concludes with questions that help you apply what you are reading.

- Develop the spiritual perspective to embrace trials
- Appreciate the maturity trials produce
- Understand the rewards for enduring trials
- Recognize God is still compassionate and gracious during trials

Enduring Trials God's Way has been endorsed by well-known ministry leaders:

- "Richly biblical and encouraging, Scott LaPierre's latest book reveals a gracious pastor's heart, compassionately equipping people for trials. Every believer needs this book!"
  Douglas Bond—Speaker, tour leader, and author
- "One of the best biblical treatments of suffering I have seen. You want this book in your library!"
  Dr. Carlton McLeod—Speaker, author, and senior pastor

A Father Offers His Son: The True and Greater Sacrifice Revealed Through Abraham and Isaac

Have you ever wondered why God asked Abraham to sacrifice his son in Genesis 22? The Angel stopped Abraham showing God did not intend for him to kill Isaac, but what did God desire? God wanted to test Abraham, and readers will discover the account primarily reveals:

- In human terms what God would do with His Son two thousand years later
- The many ways Abraham and Isaac are a picture of God and His Son
- The tremendous love of God shown through Christ's sacrifice

Endorsed by ministry leaders:

- "I highly recommend this work that will deepen your appreciation for what the Father and Son went through."
  Dr. Paul Benware—Professor, pastor, speaker, and author
- "As a jeweler holds a gemstone and examines each priceless, shining facet, Pastor Scott holds high this picture of heaven's sacrificial love and examines every detail."
  Cary Green—Senior pastor, missionary, and church planter

Notes

ⁱ Bob Black, *The Abolition of Work and Other Essays* (Port Townsend: Loompanics Unlimited, 1986).

ⁱⁱ Ronald Sailler and David Wyrtzen, *The Practice of Wisdom* (Chicago: Moody, 1992), 82.

ⁱⁱⁱ Saint Augustine, *The Works of Saint Augustine: A Translation for the 21st Century, Part 3 – Sermons,* ed. John E. Rotelle, vols. I–II (Brooklyn, NY: New City Press, 1990) s.333.2.5.

^{iv} Charles Bridges, *An Exposition of the Book of Proverbs,* (BiblioBazaar, May 20, 2009) vii.

^v Robert Frost Quotes. (n.d.). BrainyQuote.com. Retrieved June 22, 2020, from BrainyQuote.com Web site: https://www.brainyquote.com/quotes/robert_frost_122880

^{vi} F.P. Cappuccio, et al, "Sleep Duration and All-Cause Mortality: A Systematic Review and Meta-Analysis of Prospective Studies," *National Library of Medicine,* May 2010, https://www.ncbi.nlm.nih.gov/pubmed/20469800

^{vii} Warren Wiersbe, *Be Heroic,* 2nd edition (David C. Cook, 2010).

^{viii} John Calvin, *Calvin's Commentary Volume XX 1 & 2 Corinthians* (Baker Book House, 1979) 93.

^{ix} Harrison Monarth, Entrepreneur, "You've Already Abandoned Your New Year's Resolution…," January 14, 2019, https://www.entrepreneur.com/article/326096.

^x "Diligence." Dictionary.com. Accessed 22 June, 2020.

https://www.dictionary.com/browse/diligence

[xi] Warren Wiersbe, *The Bible Exposition Commentary: Wisdom and Poetry*, 2nd edition (David C. Cook, 2004), 430.

[xii] Encyclopedia of World Biography, "Thomas Alva Edison," Encyclopedia.com. (August 7, 2019). https://www.encyclopedia.com/history/encyclopedias-almanacs-transcripts-and-maps/thomas-alva-edison

xiii Benjamin Franklin, *The Way to Wealth and Poor Richard's Almanac* (Nayika Publishing, 2008), 2.

[xiv] Frank E. Gaebelein, *Expositor's Bible Commentary (Vol 5) Psalms, Proverbs, Ecclesiastes, Song of Songs* (Grand Rapids, MI: Zondervan, 1991), 973

[xv] "G3853 – paraggellō – *Strong's Greek Lexicon* (KJV)." Blue Letter Bible. Accessed 19 Aug, 2019. https://www.blueletterbible.org//lang/lexicon/lexicon.cfm?Strongs=G3853&t=KJV

[xvi] "G812 – atakteō – *Strong's Greek Lexicon* (KJV)." Blue Letter Bible. Accessed 19 Aug, 2019. https://www.blueletterbible.org//lang/lexicon/lexicon.cfm?Strongs=G812&t=KJV

[xvii] Warren Wiersbe, *Be Ready Living in Light of Christ's Return* (David C. Cook, 2010), 168.

[xviii] Charles Spurgeon, The Spurgeon Archive, Accessed 19 Aug, 2019, http://archive.spurgeon.org/misc/plowman.php

[xix] "G4874 – synanamignymi – *Strong's Greek Lexicon* (KJV)." Blue Letter Bible. Accessed 19 Aug, 2019. https://www.blueletterbible.org//lang/lexicon/lexicon.cfm?Strongs=G4874&t=KJV.

[xx] Rachel Premack. "17 Seriously Disturbing Facts about Your Job." August 2, 2018. https://www.businessinsider.com/disturbing-facts-about-your-job-2011-2

[xxi] Joel Osteen, *Your Best Life Now: 7 Steps to Living at Your Full Potential* (FaithWords, 2004), 5, 31–32, 35.

[xxii] Christine D. Johnson, "FaithWords celebrates 10 years of 'Your Best Life Now.'" Accessed 24 May 2020. https://www.christianretailing.com/index.php/newsletter/latest/27354-faithwords-celebrates-10-years-of-your-best-life-now.

[xxiii] Wyatt, Cindy. "Only One Life, Twill Soon Be Past – Poem by C.T. Studd". *Poetry About Jesus and Salvation.* Accessed 22 June, 2020. http://cavaliersonly.com/poetry_by_christian_poets_of_the_past/only_one_life_twill_soon_be_past_-_poem_by_ct_studd

[xxiv] "G1987 – epistamai – *Strong's Greek Lexicon* (KJV)." Blue Letter Bible. Accessed 9 Sep, 2019. https://www.blueletterbible.org/lang/lexicon/lexicon.cfm?t=kjv&strongs=g1987

[xxv] "G1108 – gnōsis – *Strong's Greek Lexicon* (KJV)." Blue Letter Bible. Accessed 9 Sep, 2019. https://www.blueletterbible.org/lang/Lexicon/Lexicon.cfm?strongs=G1108&t=KJV

[xxvi] "G5092 – timē– *Strong's Greek Lexicon* (KJV)." Blue Letter Bible. Accessed 10 Sep, 2019. https://www.blueletterbible.org/lang/Lexicon/Lexicon.cfm?strongs=G5092&t=KJV

[xxvii] "G1135 – gynē – *Strong's Greek Lexicon* (KJV)." Blue Letter Bible. Accessed 9 Sep, 2019. http://blueletterbible.org/lang/Lexicon/Lexicon.cfm?strongs=G1135&t=KJV

xxviii "G1134 – gynaikeios – *Strong's Greek Lexicon* (KJV)." Blue Letter Bible. Accessed 9 Sep, 2019. https://www.blueletterbible.org/lang/Lexicon/Lexicon.cfm?strongs=G1134&t=KJV

xxix "New Zealand Interschool's Weightlifting Championship 2014 – Round 6" (PDF). Sporty.co.nz. Accessed 24 May 2020. https://www.sporty.co.nz/asset/downloadasset?id=58b9b97e-f4ab-4e94-a2fe-507c024cb178

xxx Matt Windley. (19 March 2017). "Laurel Hubbard wins female 90kg+ division at weightlifting's Australian International". Herald Sun. Accessed 24 May 2020. https://www.heraldsun.com.au/sport/more-sports/laurel-hubbard-wins-female-90kg-division-at-weightliftings-australian-international/news-story/cd4a5fa012eb9a5ceb0281faceea5c7a

xxxi Miller AE; MacDougall JD; Tarnopolsky MA; Sale DG (1993). "Gender differences in strength and muscle fiber characteristics." *European Journal of Applied Physiology and Occupational Physiology*. 66 (3): 254–62.

xxxii "G1581 – ekkoptō– *Strong's Greek Lexicon* (KJV)." Blue Letter Bible. Accessed 9 Sep, 2019. https://www.blueletterbible.org/lang/Lexicon/Lexicon.cfm?strongs=G1581&t=KJV

xxxiii C. H. Spurgeon, *Sermons of the Rev. C.H. Spurgeon, of London*, Volume 20 (Sheldon, Blakeman, 1875), p. 506.

xxxiv J.R. Miller, *Secrets Of Happy Home Life: What Have You To Do With It?* (Kessinger Publishing, 1894), p. 12.

xxxv Daniela Lup, "Something to Celebrate (Or Not): The Differing Impact of Promotion to Manager on the Job Satisfaction of Women and Men," Work, Employment and Society, 32 (2). pp. 407–425

(2018), Middlesex University, accessed September 18, 2019, https://eprints.mdx.ac.uk/21841/3/WES%2520manuscript%2520f or%2520mdxrepository.pdf

xxxvi Betsey Stevenson and Justin Wolfers, "The Paradox of Declining Female Happiness," May 2009, IZA, http://ftp.iza.org/dp4200.pdf

xxxvii Zachary J, Ward, et al, "Simulation of Growth Trajectories of Childhood Obesity into Adulthood," *New England Journal of Medicine*, November 30, 2017, https://www.nejm.org/doi/full/10.1056/NEJMoa1703860

xxxviii "Childhood Obesity Causes and Consequences," Centers for Disease Control and Prevention, Accessed September 1, 2019, https://www.cdc.gov/obesity/childhood/causes.html

xxxix Claire McCarthy, "More Than Half of Today's Children Will Be Obese Adults," Harvard Health Publishing – Harvard Medical School, December 5, 2017, https://www.health.harvard.edu/blog/more-than-half-of-todays-children-will-be-obese-adults-2017120512879

xl T. J. Horton, et al, "Fat and Carbohydrate Overfeeding in Humans: Different Effects on Energy Storage," *American Journal of Clinical Nutrition* (1995) 62 (1): 19–29.

xli ABC News, "Rachel Canning Loses Effort to Make Parents Pay High School Tuition," Accessed 26 May 2020. https://abcnews.go.com/US/rachel-canning-loses-suit-make-parents-pay-high/story?id=22768908

xlii "Child sues parents for posting 'embarrassing' baby pictures on social media" October 29, 2016. https://www.cbc.ca/radio/thisisthat/selfie-kid-graffiti-counselor-golf-course-accidental-pianist-1.3811185/child-sues-parents-for-posting-embarrassing-baby-pictures-on-social-media-1.3811188

xliii World News Daily Report, "17-Year-Old Teenager Sues His Parents for Being Born White" Accessed June 18, 2020. https://worldnewsdailyreport.com/17-year-old-teenager-sues-his-parents-for-being-born-white/

xliv Cary, Otis, and Frank Cary. "How Old Were Christ's Disciples?" *The Biblical World*, vol. 50, no. 1, 1917, pp. 3–12. *JSTOR*, www.jstor.org/stable/3136128. Accessed 28 May 2020.

xlv "Stress…At Work," Centers for Disease Control and Prevention – National Institute for Occupational Safety and Health, https://www.cdc.gov/niosh/docs/99-101/.

xlvi Colleen de Bellefonds, "7 Red Flags You're Working Too Much," Healthline, Accessed 19 Aug, 2019 https://www.healthline.com/health/working-too-much-health-effects#4

xlvii Gordon T. McInnes, "Overtime Is Bad for the Heart," *European Heart Journal,* May 11, 2010, http://eurheartj.oxfordjournals.org/content/31/14/1672.long

xlviii Susan Donaldson James, "Working Too Hard? Job Stress Doubles Depression Risk, Study Says," *ABC News,* January 26, 2012, https://abcnews.go.com/Health/working-hard-increase-risk-major-depression-british-study/story?id=15442607

xlix Marianna Virtanen, et al, "Overtime Work as a Predictor of Major Depressive Episode: A 5-Year Follow-up of the Whitehall II Study," Plos One, January 25, 2012, http://journals.plos.org/plosone/article?id=10.1371/journal.pone.0030719

l Amanda L. Chan, "Overtime Linked With Higher Depression: Risk: Study," Huffington Post, Updated March 27, 2012,

https://www.huffpost.com/entry/overtime-work-depression_n_1234025

li John Pencavel, "The Productivity of Working Hours," The Institute for the Study of Labor, April 2014, http://ftp.iza.org/dp8129.pdf

lii John MacArthur, *The MacArthur Bible Commentary* (Thomas Nelson, 2005), 1446.

liii John MacArthur, *The MacArthur Bible Commentary* (Thomas Nelson, 2005), 1477.

liv Matthew Henry, *Matthew Henry's Commentary: In One Volume* (Zondervan, 1961), p. 1716.

lv Rachel Nall, et al, "How Does Seven to Eight Hours of Sleep Affect Your Body?" Healthline, Accessed 19 Aug, 2019, https://www.healthline.com/health/science-sleep-why-you-need-7-8-hours-night

lvi Francesco P. Cappuccio, et al, "Sleep Duration and All-Cause Mortality: A Systemic Review and Meta-Analysis of Prospective Studies,", U.S. National Library of Medicine, May 2, 2010 https://www.ncbi.nlm.nih.gov/pmc/articles/PMC2864873/

lvii H.R. Colten and B.M. Altevogt eds. "Sleep Disorders and Sleep Deprivation: An Unmet Public Health Problem," U.S. National Library of Medicine, 2006, https://www.ncbi.nlm.nih.gov/pubmed/20669438

lviii P.M. Nilsson, et al. "Incidence of Diabetes in Middle-Aged Men Is Related to Sleep Disturbances," *Diabetes Care.* 2004; 27(10): 2464.

lix Gottlieb DJ, et al. Association of Sleep Time with Diabetes Mellitus and Impaired Glucose Tolerance, *Archives of Internal Medicine.* 2005 Apr 25; 165(8): 863.

[lx] K.L. Knutson, et al. "Role of Sleep Duration and Quality in the Risk and Severity of Type 2 Diabetes Mellitus," *Archives of Internal Medicine.* 2006 Sep 18; 166(16):1768.

[lxi] N. D. Kohatsu, et al. "Sleep Duration and Body Mass Index in a Rural Population," *Archives of Internal Medicine.* 2006 Sep 18; 166(16): 1701.

[lxii] S. Taheri, L. et al, "Short Sleep Duration Is Associated with Reduced Leptin, Elevated Ghrelin, and Increased Body Mass Index," U.S. National Library of Medicine, December 13, 2004, https://www.ncbi.nlm.nih.gov/pubmed/15602591

[lxiii] E.M. Taveras, et al. "Short Sleep Duration in Infancy and Risk of Childhood Overweight," *Archives of Pediatrics & Adolescent Medicine.* 2008 Apr; 162(4): 305.

[lxiv] "Surprising Reasons to Get More Sleep," WebMD, Accessed 20 Aug 2019, https://www.webmd.com/sleep-disorders/benefits-sleep-more

[lxv] C.R. King, et al. "Short Sleep Duration and Incident Coronary Artery Calcification," *Journal of the American Medical Association*, 2008: 300(24): 2859–2866.

[lxvi] "Sleep, Learning, and Memory" Division of Sleep Medicine, Harvard Medical School, December 18, 2007, http://healthysleep.med.harvard.edu/healthy/matters/benefits-of-sleep/learning-memory

[lxvii] M.P. Walker, et al, "Cognitive Flexibility Across the Sleep-Wake Cycle: REM-Sleep Enhancement of Anagram Problem Solving," U.S. National Library of Medicine, November 14, 2002, https://www.ncbi.nlm.nih.gov/pubmed/12421655

[lxviii] M. Irwin, et al, "Partial Night Sleep Deprivation Reduces

Natural Killer and Cellular Immune Responses in Humans," U.S. National Library of Medicine, April 10, 1996, https://www.ncbi.nlm.nih.gov/pubmed/8621064

[lxix] S. Cohen, et al. "Sleep Habits and Susceptibility to the Common Cold," *Archives of Internal Medicine* 2009 Jan 12; 169 (1):62–67.

[lxx] "Six for 2006: Six Reasons Not to Scrimp on Sleep" *Harvard Women's Health Watch*, Vol 13 No 5 (January 2006), https://www.tamaqua.k12.pa.us/cms/lib07/PA01000119/Centricity/Domain/108/sleep.pdf

[lxxi] E. van der Helm, N. Gujar, and M.P. Walker, "Sleep Deprivation Impairs the Accurate Recognition of Human Emotions,", U.S. National Library of Medicine, March 2010 https://www.ncbi.nlm.nih.gov/pubmed/20337191

[lxxii] Robson, David, "The Disgusting Secrets of Smelly Feet," BBC Future, July 31, 2015, http://www.bbc.com/future/story/20150730-the-disgusting-secrets-of-smelly-feet

[lxxiii] Warren Wiersbe, *Bible Exposition Commentary, Vol 1: New Testament* (Chariot Victor Publishing, 2003), 213.

[lxxiv] "Willow Creek Repents," Christianity Today, Inc. October 18, 2007, https://www.christianitytoday.com/pastors/2007/october-online-only/willow-creek-repents.html

[lxxv] "G4049 – perispaō – Strong's Greek Lexicon (KJV)." Blue Letter Bible. Accessed 21 Aug, 2019, https://www.blueletterbible.org//lang/Lexicon/Lexicon.cfm?Strongs=G4049&t=KJV

[lxxvi] Cogley, Richard W. *John Eliot's Mission to the Indians Before King Philip's War.* (Cambridge, Mass: Harvard University Press, 1999).

lxxvii John F. MacArthur, *Hebrews: Christ: Perfect Sacrifice, Perfect Priest* (Thomas Nelson, June 28, 2016), 20.

lxxviii "G3870 – parakaleō – Strong's Greek Lexicon (KJV)." Blue Letter Bible. Accessed 19 Aug, 2019. https://www.blueletterbible.org//lang/lexicon/lexicon.cfm?Strongs=G3870&t=KJV

lxxix Gordon J. Wenham, *World Biblical Commentary, Genesis 1–15* (Thomas Nelson, 1987), 80–81.

lxxx Michael Rydelink, *The Moody Bible Commentary* New edition (Moody Bible Publishers, February 2014), 1927.

lxxxi "G4520 – sabbatismos – *Strong's Greek Lexicon* (KJV)." Blue Letter Bible. Accessed 19 Aug, 2019. https://www.blueletterbible.org//lang/lexicon/lexicon.cfm?Strongs=G4520&t=KJV

lxxxii "G2664 – katapauō – *Strong's Greek Lexicon* (KJV)." Blue Letter Bible. Accessed 19 Aug, 2019. https://www.blueletterbible.org//lang/lexicon/lexicon.cfm?Strongs=G2664&t=KJV

lxxxiii "G2041 – ergon – *Strong's Greek Lexicon* (KJV)." Blue Letter Bible. Accessed 19 Aug, 2019. https://www.blueletterbible.org/lang/Lexicon/Lexicon.cfm?strongs=G2041&t=KJV

lxxxiv "356 Prophecies Fulfilled in Jesus Christ." According to the Scriptures, Accessed 19 Aug, 2019. http://www.accordingtothescriptures.org/prophecy/353prophecies.html

lxxxv Joni Eareckson Tada, "A Deeper Healing," Grace to You, October 13, 2013, https://www.gty.org/library/sermons-library/TM13-2/a-deeper-healing-joni-eareckson-tada

[lxxxvi] Joni Eareckson Tada, "Why Joni Eareckson Tada Praises God for not Healing Her," The Gospel Coalition, July 17, 2019, https://www.thegospelcoalition.org/article/joni-earekson-tada-praises-healing/

Made in the USA
San Bernardino, CA
11 August 2020

76962073R00135